GRIMETHORPE
REVIVAL

Front cover: photographs by kind permission of Lynda Bellingham,
Nick Yates, RANKIN, Alison Steadman, Gary Clark, Stephen Buckley
and the Clegg Family (from top left to right).
Back cover: Amelia Watson, Jim Moran & *Yorkshire Post Newspapers.*
Background images: Mark Britton and John Britton.

GRIMETHORPE REVIVAL

Celebrity Support
for a Coalfield Community

MEL DYKE

Wharncliffe Books

First published in Great Britain in 2013 by
Wharncliffe Books
an imprint of
Pen and Sword Books Ltd
47 Church Street
Barnsley
South Yorkshire S70 2AS

ISBN 978 1 84563 152 9

Printed and bound in England by
CPI Group (UK) Ltd, Croydon, CR0 4YY

Typeset in Sabon by CHIC GRAPHICS

Pen & Sword Books Ltd incorporates the imprints of
Pen & Sword Aviation, Pen & Sword Family History, Pen & Sword Maritime,
Pen & Sword Military, Pen & Sword Discovery, Wharncliffe Local History,
Wharncliffe True Crime, Wharncliffe Transport, Pen & Sword Select,
Pen & Sword Military Classics, Leo Cooper, Remember When,
The Praetorian Press, Seaforth Publishing and Frontline Publishing

For a complete list of Pen and Sword titles please contact
Pen and Sword Books Limited
47 Church Street, Barnsley, South Yorkshire, S70 2AS, England
E-mail: enquiries@pen-and-sword.co.uk
Website: www.pen-and-sword.co.uk

Contents

Foreword

There are people you meet in life who you never forget. Mel Dyke is one of those people. While others shy away from the media, Mel embraces it... and with good reason. She has cracking stories to tell and man is she able to tell them! Charismatic, creative yet truly grounded, she was, and remains, an interviewer's gift. She is a 'personality' in the true meaning of the word.

Years ago Mel introduced me to the play *Children of the Dark* performed by the pupils of The Oaks School in Barnsley where she was deputy head. It told the story of Victorian children killed and injured in a mining disaster that led to reform of child labour laws.

The young school performers I had the privilege of seeing drew from the tragedies of the past for artistic expression just as another shadow was looming over coalfields in the form of pit closures. Inspired by Mel, those youngsters were shining examples of how art can illuminate the darkest times. I know she is deeply grateful to the many influential women who helped turn a national spotlight on the endeavours of The Oaks and then Grimethorpe schoolchildren especially in their efforts to highlight the predicament of girls living in communities so dependent on the coal industry. They include Elizabeth Peacock, Maureen Lipman, Lynda Bellingham, Betty Boothroyd, Kate Adie and Mo Mowlam to name just a few.

I once had an extraordinary teacher who made me believe that my dreams and ambitions were achievable. In her words and actions Mel reveals that she has a kindred heart. If there were guardians of the spirit of Yorkshire she would certainly be among them.

Mike McCarthy

Special Acknowledgements

The true writers of this book are listed in the final pages. They are colleagues, teachers, pupils, journalists, producers, directors, friends, comparative strangers and superstars, each of whom has made a generous contribution. Without their inputs, whenever and in whatever form, there would be no book. My sincere thanks go to all of them. I have wherever possible attempted to credit everyone although especially with former pupils that has not always been possible or appropriate. I hope and trust that any unforeseen omission is not taken as ingratitude.

I am though particularly indebted to the following for ongoing support without which an end result would not have been possible:

All members of the highly professional and skilled Pen & Sword team, in particular Charles Hewitt, Jonathan Wright, Sylvia Menzies-Earl, Kirsty Williams and Matt Jones for their smiling responses even on bad days.

Brian Elliott for his unfailing editorial advice and friendship.

James Britton, who takes the endurance award for his patience and expertise, in ensuring my still pathetic lack of skill on a computer did not lose the entire book on more than one occasion.

John Britton, for generously giving time he couldn't spare, restoring and photographing old faxes, photographs and newspaper cuttings, to a legible condition.

Elizabeth Ellis, Christiane Rich, Mimi Watson, India Watson and David Clapham, who over the past three years have collated, helped research or copy the material.

My son Tim Dyke, and my daughter Stephanie Watson, who are a constant source of reassurance and energy through their unfailing support, individual skills and shared ideas.

My grandchildren, George and Charlie Dyke, Mimi, India and Benny Watson, all long distance Reds' supporters, remain proud of the links they have with Barnsley's mining and glassblowing past, in their great and great great grandfathers respectively.

For her generosity of spirit, wise counsel and encouragement, Jess Clegg, who suggested putting this material together, and the sheer delight of whose company I miss so much.

Introduction

1992 was the year Her Majesty The Queen referred to as, an *annus horribilis*. It wasn't that good a year for Grimethorpe either, when the announcement was made that its pit was one of thirty-one coal mines to be closed as part of the Government's new Energy Policy. Ironically, Grimethorpe Colliery Band that year was hailed as the best in the world, after winning the World Brass Band Championship. The Band survives to the present day, but Grimethorpe's ninety-nine-year-old rich-seamed pit did not. Failure to conduct the statutory 'consultation period' of ninety days led to no real review but merely delayed the actual closure date to 7 May 1993, with much of the population seemingly blithely unaware that the end of those thirty-one pits would also end a traditional way of life for the communities they supported.

A Barnsley miner's daughter, working in schools and colleges in the coalfields from the late 1960s is where this story starts. Massive support from positive role models across the arts and using the area's mining history, when the 1992 closures announcement came, I was working as a Deputy Head in a Grimethorpe school, enabled by a creative counter movement to fight for children's educational aspirations and dreams. The local community was instantly involved, then national and finally international support came though. But no-one would have predicted the depth of emotion in a range of responses from Westminster Abbey to Sheffield Cathedral, the House of Commons to Buckingham Palace, London's West End to Emmerdale and from an artichoke field in France to Coronation Street.

An unprecedented range of left, right and centre political and other goodwill messages fortified the community motivating children's writing and other activities across the curriculum at a seemingly hopeless moment time for mining communities. The result was a unique archive of those diverse memories, television, radio, media reports, letters, interviews, stories, photographs and diaries from MPs, clerics, academics, actors, artists and other celebrities some of whom remain involved to the present day.

Catching up with some of those children and their famous supporters twenty years on, provides a comprehensive insight into previously underplayed or unpublished perspectives and memories. Through their occasionally heartbreaking but often inspirational stories we see how some have not simply survived the destruction of their community, but actually triumphed over it.

Chapter 1

Long Eaton to Scawsby
1906–1978

It seems to me that it was on a day in 1906 that a significant revolution in education actually began, in the small mining town of Long Eaton, Derbyshire. In 1899 the school leaving age had been raised to twelve years, and was followed by the Education Act of 1902 which abolishing the old school boards then established local educational authorities which were also to be responsible for building and maintaining schools. Routine inspection of and reporting on those Elementary Schools was undertaken and it was on such a visit that one School Inspector, Michael Sadler, observed a young teacher Sam Clegg 'who poured his personality into the service of a small industrialised community and by his genius and good sense made his school a focus of inspiration and creative force'. Clearly inspired himself, Sadler's official report glowingly described him as 'high voltage cable' which in motivating this new generation of learners actually 'vivified and electrified the whole community'.

This radical approach of teaching beyond the 3Rs through the arts also presented practical opportunities for the youngsters to develop skills which would in turn prepare them for such alternative work as was available locally, in lace-making. A century later, nationwide we would form task groups, sub-committees and working parties to discuss employers' similar needs and 'invent' a National Skills Agenda. From that earlier meeting of minds, one man's recognition of another's creative vision and philosophy, resulted six years later in Sam Clegg, being appointed Head of the new custom-built Long Eaton Elementary School. This educational development in recognising and catering for the needs of local industry, provided a workforce already semi-skilled, and placed the Arts at the fore when a combination of both technical and community education was born.

It's just possible that building schools for the future began then too!

With his appointment as Head of a new school to replace the old, Sam Clegg's influence ensured that the new building matched his methodology. Built around a centrally focussed glass Arts studio, the atmosphere was outward-looking, bright and light with like-minded staff. Expansion of his 'modern methods' sowed seeds, which literally through his only son Alec, and his eldest daughter Mary, would develop a dynasty which would change the face of education. Alec Clegg's tenure as Director of Education in the West Riding of Yorkshire brought not only a similar extensive building program, but a quality of teaching development which in the latter half of the twentieth century marked the county as a centre of educational excellence. His own potential was even more enhanced by Jess, his wife, who in acquainting me with Robert Bridges, to sum up their philosophy had no idea that it was also a perfect description of her:

'...of almost all minds and hearts to win, new beauty of soul from the embrace of beauty and strength by practised combat against folly and wrong'.

An inspirational teacher – Jess Clegg, wife of Sir Alec Clegg. Photograph by kind permission of the Clegg family.

One former pupil-teacher at Long Eaton, F L Attenborough, went up to Emmanuel College Cambridge in 1915. By 1919, specialising in Anglo-Saxon Studies, he had become a Fellow of Emmanuel and was working on what is still recognised as one of the most highly regarded texts in his field. 1992 saw publication of that work, *The Laws of the Earliest English Kings,* and his marriage to Sam Clegg's daughter Mary.

Formerly Head of History at Clegg's newly built Scawsby College of Education, D K Jones joined the School of Education staff at the University of Leicester in 1972 when living memories still regaled with tales of the days of 'Prinnie'.

Jones' continuing interest and research brings interesting glimpses of the man:

'If, as Principal of the University he helped to create, Freddy Attenborough happened to be walking on the site where an informal game of football was going on, it was more than likely the ball would be kicked his way with a shout of 'Head this one Prinnie!'

It was first as Principal of a Training College in Isleworth that F L Attenborough's capabilities and leadership resulted in it becoming one of the best known colleges in the country. By 1932 he had become the second Principal of Leicester's eleven-year-old University College where he found real local enthusiasm for the institution; but he also found it struggling for financial support. His academic and administrative skills again came into play with finalisation of long sought recognition of the college as a centre for the one year graduate teacher-training course. The perennial student fees issue was addressed as a priority and within six years twenty-four bursaries and ten scholarships had been awarded suggesting that Attenborough's advice to his own sons was as readily applied to others. There was an early ambience between departments and Education was not seen as peripheral, as sadly it still is in some other institutions. Maybe Sam Clegg's early influence is reflected in Jack Simmons' tribute to Attenborough's leadership on his retirement through ill health in 1951:

'He had left his mark most notably by the care he showed for the aesthetic standards of everything connected with it. The modern universities have not been rich in such men. Too often they have been content with the ugly and the dull, in paint and printing and furniture and architecture, because no one has taken the trouble to insist on something better. Mr Attenborough took that trouble with happy results for the College... Most important of all he brought to his office two of the qualities that at that stage it needed most; steady enthusiasm and patience in adversity.'

Alan Blackhurst, a former student, recalls:

'Here you were in the post war period when things were beginning to happen. It was as good a time as you could imagine. There was a prevailing sense of liberalism, a tolerance – characterised by Attenborough.'

Those attributes were critical in securing the subsequent Privy Council Royal Charter, which finally resulted in the college being awarded University status in 1957 after failing health brought on F L Attenborough's early retirement. Jones' own judgement is:

'What can be stated is that in 1951 although much remained to be done in preparation for independence before success was achieved, Attenborough had presided over the laying of the foundation of an independent university and ensured that the institution would not be diverted from this goal. It was indeed a triumphant life.'

Intuitively working to what was also the BBC's original charter – to inform, to educate and to entertain – the Attenborough family's influence on education is inestimable. Sam Clegg's daughter Mary, still spoken of with utmost respect and affection and a strong supporter of theatre, was for many years Chair of the Leicester Little Theatre which, formerly Leicester Amateur Theatre Group, opened the year they arrived and is where eldest son Richard first appeared. Watch any one of Richard Attenborough's films whether as actor, director or producer for the full range of social history. From the outset there was invariably a moral or a sting in the tale taking the alternative stance, as his chilling thug psychopathic gang mentality in *Brighton Rock* in 1946 is followed by 1949 *Boys in Brown* depicting life in a Borstal institution. The anti capital punishment in *10 Rillington Place* is moderated by barefaced mockery of the justice system in *Dock Brief*.

4

1948's *The Guinea Pig* brought early exposure of the problems encountered by bright children from working class families trying to fit into 'better' schools after winning scholarship places. *I'm Alright Jack* treats a post war rise of trade unionism as comedy, and then hits back more dramatically in 1960 with *An Angry Silence*. Or you can choose between sheer delight in productions such as his *Whistle Down the Wind* or revive international hostility from World War Two right through to his epic 1982 *Ghandi* with his 2007 *Closing the Ring* whether by design or intent doing exactly that, embracing lives and loves to the latest 'troubles' in Ireland.

If you prefer TV, consider award winning series of televisual history, and try to recall at exactly what point in *Life* you realised that you were being lulled by a false sense of entertainment, albeit at the highest level. Did you ever actually realise that whilst doing just that by his magical sleight of intellect and personal charm, David Attenborough had also furthered your education by totally engaging you in subjects you had once opted out of at school? Teaching by stealth, and we love it still. A veritable lifetime of achievement deserving every award he has won in sixty years of family education where every generation is still informed, educated and entertained.

The author at an interview with Sir David Attenborough.

I suspect his favourite aunt was Jess Clegg who likened him to a another description she gave me of his grandfather Sam Clegg:

'... a radical pioneer, a stringent and stimulating teacher, an undaunted soul. When you had once seen him and felt the charm and fire in his mind you never forgot him.'

Nearly fifty years after 'Cleggery', Barnsley was still where geographically it had always been, in the West Riding of Yorkshire, but outside its separate educational provision. Since 1944/5 the mighty West Riding County Council's Director of Education had been Alec Clegg. Born of this family of natural educators, his views and philosophy for the development of education were equally revolutionary in the years following the 1944 Education Act. His empathic perception of the needs of children from disadvantaged backgrounds, so far removed from his own, was no less revolutionary than that of his father had been half a century earlier.

Amongst his initiatives were many which would impact on awareness of the Arts and in particular the provision for future training of teachers in the Arts. Woolley Hall was redeveloped as a centre for in-service training of existing teachers. Bretton Hall became the centre for undergraduate and postgraduate trainee teachers in the Arts. By the 1960s a school building in Swinton was adapted to be used to set up a course to take on mature students with five or more good O Level passes back into higher education to train as teachers. And I had just begun to realise how much of my own time in the years of my 'formal education' had been wasted.

With a good family support system and my two children now settled at the nearby junior school, I responded to the advertisement in the *Barnsley Chronicle* for Clegg's teacher-training course. As a lower school pupil a decision had been unilaterally taken that I should not be included in the groups to study Maths to O level standard. Neither I nor my parents had understood that the subsequent lack of that qualification could seriously impact on my future educational and career prospects, including teaching. However, despite not having the prerequisite qualification in Maths, it was decided at my interview that as I was applying to teach English, and had worked in a bank prior to my marriage, that experience would suffice as an alternative. I doubt it would by today's automated selection procedures, but that system was based on flexible intelligence rather than tick boxes, on developing potential strengths rather than identifying weaknesses. So in 1966 I was allowed to begin the three year Advanced Main Course at what would soon become Scawsby College of Higher Education.

It was in the English Department on that course that I first became aware of an 1839 Royal Commission set up to enquire into conditions in coal mining. Under the leadership of Dr Donald McKelvie and Clifford Laycock, the respective Heads of the college's English and Drama Departments, students performed a play for voices based on the findings of that Commission. It was harrowing but compulsive in its revelation of the part that miners local to the area had played in an historic tragedy, and the subsequent introduction of improvements in working conditions in that industry. It would be five years before I could present a full and public version of that piece of history across the boundaries of a school's curriculum, but well worth the wait.

In 1972 the 1968 Act raising the school leaving age from fifteen years of age was implemented meaning that it was a requirement for all children to attend school until they were sixteen. At that time Horace Crowther, recently head-hunted from a Clegg school in the West Riding, newly appointed Headteacher, asked me to set up an Individual Needs Unit at Darton High School, intended to enable all children leaving that school to read and write sufficiently well to facilitate the requirements of the posts they would take up as full time employment. As statistically the boys had been underperforming, they became a priority in pro-active management of the predictable problems.

Mining was the obvious choice for many of the boys, but a stumbling block was the need to evidence ability to read the safety notices underground. These were still in the antiquated Victorian language form in which they were first introduced in the Mines and Colliery Act of 1843 and required a reading age ability higher than might have been anticipated for many of these youngsters. One of my first tasks was to overcome this hindrance and with immense support from Ian Barr then Manager of Woolley Colliery, we first arranged underground visits, and then a set of basic requirements for the lads to aim for. A good school attendance record, reports indicating good behaviour and sound knowledge of the safety procedures underground were to set the standard, which would guarantee them an interview. If their records were deemed satisfactory the offer of a place on one of the NCB's new, and highly desirable, apprenticeship schemes would be open to them. My original concerns that they might think their macho image might be adversely affected if they

The Children of the Dark: *performed at Darton High School 1974. Cast members from the left front row: Andrew Strutt, Jeremy Dawson, John Storrs, Robert Teale, Michael Pollard, Alan Foster. Second row from left: Simon Worth, Ian Collins, John Schofield, Jill Galloway, Nicky Porter, Jean Lloyd, Hilary Ball. Staff from left: M A Bould, Gavin Sturgess, Mel Dyke, Les Jones, seated Nick Crompton. Identified by contemporaries: Pauline Senior, Caroline Bowes, Susan Phillips, Anita Holland, Marilyn Taylor, Debbie Cook and Robert Teale.*

attended extra reading classes were soon allayed. By making them mentors to younger boys they felt secure with the task and in helping them improved their own reading skills. It took off like a rocket with an unlikely interest in the new reading scheme, which was based on irregular spellings of words such as 'alighting and boarding stations'. 'Why don't they just put get on and get off? We all know what that means!' asked one young man in all sincerity.

These experiences provided the perfect opportunity to use the Arts as another perspective to consider mining history. The ensuing increased interest in mining and its history brought the chance I had been waiting for to produce a dramatic performance of the Commissioners' report into the 1838 tragedy at Silkstone. Keen pupils and highly supportive colleagues ensured the first production of *Children of the Dark* in the school was a great success.

It was at that time that I also discovered for myself that using positive role models to inspire local children, with restricted aspiration and little if any ambition, to strive for greater achievements does work.

Eric Jackson, who we would now call an entrepreneur, was a successful

Barnsley-born business man, with a good reputation as an entertaining speaker. He accepted my invitation to visit the school to talk about his headline-making experiences as a rally car driver. Through his magical touch they discovered a new map, hearing of days a ship sailed out from Cairo through the Mediterranean, sighting every passing country en route to Capetown. Then, totally enthralled, they were with him in the rally car as he described his own fight against time and the dangers of racing overland the entire length of Africa to beat it by car. I can still see the faces of those teenagers, eyes and ears glued listening to stories they wished were their own – and one day might be. More importantly, just a couple of years ago one of them reminded me of his own memories of it including the question he personally had asked his hero on that day – nearly forty years earlier.

Another favourite was Bill Atack, Managing Director of what was then Lord Kagan's Gannex empire. He caught the attention of every boy watching out of the Library windows awaiting his arrival when he pulled in to the school car park in an open-top white Mercedes. A rather attractive Personal Assistant accompanying him also caught the girls' attention as mental notes were rapidly made on their urgent need to check up on Shorthand and Typing Courses at 'Barnsley Tech'. The lads were certainly paying attention too as Atack warned them that few people were lucky enough to start work in such a good job before describing his own first experience of work at the age of fourteen, 'sweeping the floors in a tailor's shop in Leeds'.

I saw aspiration grow that day as our visitors drove off and I overheard one of the lads say, 'I'm going to have one of them one day!'

'A white convertible?' I asked naively, to his instant response 'NO! One of them PA lasses!'

The visit did have other outcomes. Whilst there was a thriving sewing industry in Barnsley at that time, there were fewer opportunities in the woollen sector. Gannex was booming, paying good wages and looking to provide training and hence career prospects for girls. Bill Atack's visit was also a recruitment drive. Girls about to leave school and in some cases their mothers too were offered jobs with staff buses provided to transport them from Kexborough and Darton to Elland. Beneficial to both sides, there was a quick take-up of the opportunity, the success of which was for me the beginning of a personal interest in stepping up the motivation of girls in the work place. It was also when I fully realised that a vital element in that motivation towards the maximisation of a child's potential, was having prospects: a future with a job.

Chapter 2

The Oaks
1978–1989

It was following such effective involvements as those that leaving Darton in 1978 was a wrench. The Oaks School in Kendray was in a state of reorganisation following the retirement of the former long serving Head and the appointment of a new one: Tony Kent. His aims to raise profile, attendance and performance matched my own, leading to my initial brief as the new female Deputy Head. As absenteeism was a major issue it became my designated priority and Keith Ellis was the first to join a team of influential locals invited into school to help raise levels of attendance and hence achievement across the board. Sergeant Ellis' work in creating a forceful juvenile liaison system now across the entire borough had gained recognition nationally bringing him a well deserved British Empire Medal. Local magistrates, a series of Education Welfare Officers, with Chairman of the Juvenile Magistrates Bench Keith Goddard and Leader of the Labour Group Cllr Fred Lunn, attended pastoral meetings in school and took the system across their own networks.

Not everyone was convinced of the value or even purpose of multi professional partnership of course. An odd one here and there in Social Services saw an invasion of client confidentiality, an unwelcome invasion of their territory or an increasing case load, so was reluctant to become engaged but Wilf Slade, Director of Social Services, saw the whole picture as did the wonderfully professional George Hunter then Chair of Barnsley Samaritans. At her lowest ebb, a seriously abused wife and son had gone missing so a discreet attendance check was in place. They had left home for school at 7 30am before 'he' was aware; the boy was in class and she remained with us until collaborative support ensured they could be taken to place of safety.

Education Welfare Officers, many bringing other professional skills from previous experience, were particularly strong in reducing absenteeism; their role was key in the move to increase standards as were the introduction of, high standards of dress and behaviour codes including contractual parental cooperation. A uniform was another priority in a catchment which included both affluent and seriously deprived areas. Children wearing grey pullovers and skirts or trousers whilst others were in denims or a range of trendy clothes was both divisive and embarrassing.

Within the school itself some were slower than others to breach traditional academic or pastoral boundaries, but the ethos became exceptionally supportive of some massive needs, especially during times of unemployment or strikes. Craft teacher John Whittington would willingly do repairs on children's shoes in the department. One doubly enuretic child's personal hygiene problem became so extreme that after fruitless attempts by all agencies, Social Services provided a second school uniform to be kept in school along with bath towels. Matron volunteered to come to school half an hour early every day to open the showers enabling the girl to change into her fresh uniform every day and no-one was aware.

As Co Deputy Head, Gordon Simpson was promoted to a Headship in Oldham, his place was taken by Terry Mullen whose appointment further reflected Tony Kent's purpose in raising academic standards in line with his own subject specialism, Modern Foreign Languages. Already Chief Moderator for Mathematics with the Yorkshire Board, which was at that time one of five northern CSE Boards, Mullen was the obvious choice to represent Yorkshire in a new alliance of the five, the Northern Examination Association. Subsequent increased involvement in the development and introduction of a 'brand new' examination, the General Certificate of Secondary Education in 1986, by which time he was Chair of Mathematics for the whole NEA Board, not only increased standards of staff training at national level but provided additional expertise across the whole LEA and exceptionally for the school. His inclusion as NEA representative on the Schools' Examination and Assessment Council prior to the implementation of the National Curriculum ensured that the school was well ahead of the game. He then joined Prof Hugh Burkhart's team on the Nottingham University-based Numeracy Project. This initiative was to provide new materials and interesting ways to engage lower ability fifteen and sixteen year olds in Mathematics. The Oaks became a pilot school producing its own materials leading not only internally, but created a popular and well used model that was and remains a great success.

Further pilot work continued with the Northern Partnership for Records of Achievement (NPRA). Work at The Oaks in this area was different to the other NPRA schools in that the work started in Year 7 rather than in Year 10 – enabling the whole school to benefit from its inception. The basic theme required staff to break their work down into modules with an end result rewarded by an NPRA Certificate. These short pieces fitted well into all of the Arts subjects.

In parallel with Terry Mullen, Tony Kent became Chair of NEA Modern Foreign Languages in 1985 to lead the development work for the new GCSE which was due to start in 1988. As with GCSE Maths, The Oaks became the lead school in Barnsley for In-Service Training in Modern Foreign Languages with all MFL Heads of Department and Staff including the Barnsley MFL Adviser. Kent was also invited to play a national part in syllabus approval, firstly for all Exam Boards' GCSE French examinations. It then became clear that other main languages needed extra work and he was asked to approve the German main syllabuses for Midlands Exam Group, Southern Exam Group and London East Anglia Group. It was vital to share all this national information so that The Oaks and Barnsley could become major benefactors.

In addition to these developments, after I was invited to be a part of the official Barnsley MBC delegation to Russia in 1884, the school was one of only two in the Authority to be the first to include Russian to its range of Modern Foreign Languages.

The increasing academic success combined with whole school involvement in, attendance, parental contracts and behavioural strategies led to an increase in grades across the board. So it became easy to work with outside groups and children were involved in activities unique in the area at that time.

An artist in residence helped the Arts department's community project in designing and building a Zen Garden in the grounds of Kendray Hospital near the Psychiatric and Geriatric Wards. The location provided stimulation and interest for the patients whilst developing not simply children's skills in the work but an improving awareness of the difficulties those patients had which in turn continued and improved relationships with a community group of elderly residents near to the school. On completion the garden was formally opened by HRH The Duchess of Kent.

It was the miners' strike of 1984 bringing new issues of political history which would really impact across the curriculum and the catchment area. For much of that academic year seconded to the Schools' Psychological

Students and staff of The Oaks welcome HRH The Duchess of Kent to the formal opening of the Zen Garden.

Service I was based in the old Barnsley Beckett Hospital building across the road from the NUM Headquarters. The increased footfall over there was a silent and early indicator that in the year of Orgreave, whilst much of the rest of the country, and the world, would not become aware until 2012, all was not as it seemed. Visiting every school in the borough was also a part of the seconded job so my perspective of the mood and impact was more widely based. Back in The Oaks, parents' accounts of harassment, false arrest and misrepresentation were too common to be disregarded. The now successful pastoral system we had set up in the early years really came in to play now as times worsened for virtually everyone. Stress mounted as incomes fell impacting on local businesses as well as those on strike. Occasional teenage inability to understand financial problems caused family rows bringing parents into school more frequently, but support was pulled in from every direction and connection. Staff and friends brought outgrown clothes, shoes or unwanted gifts of soap or creams, my own daughter who was by then working as cabin crew for an airline with daily access to duty free bargains, supplied cigarettes. Although a smoker, I never smoked on school premises, but did then keep a stock in my office for stressed parents who couldn't stop the habit. Professional or not, it helped us though a few tricky situations.

As ever, a sense of support and order in school remained a pre-requisite and we needed a strong alternative focus. The Oaks Pit Disaster in 1866 was one of the worst ever recorded in the history of coal mining with 361 casualties in conditions so bad that unknown numbers of unrescued bodies remain to this day entombed underground. As the memorial erected to the rescuers was in our catchment area near to the old pit site, and with families in school whose forebears had been involved in that tragedy, it was inevitable that some recognition of the 120th anniversary would be appropriate. So a new production of *Children of the Dark* was soon underway. The school's multi-talented new Head of English, Dick Walker, also played in a popular local folk band *Off the Cuff* with Andy Crothers, David Duke, and Eric Pressley. He came up with the brilliant idea and offer of getting them involved and turning it into a history-based musical. His subsequent inclusion of local vocalist Betty Martin singing new songs written by the group along with traditional songs added a new dimension and quality beyond the expectation of any school to its already excellent

Kenny Doughty, on the right, makes his first public stage appearance.

Music and Drama Departments; and now international film actor and producer, Kenny Doughty, had his first public starring role.

To add to the atmosphere of children being in a pitch black mine it was decided that when some of our children recounted the real live experiences of children from the nineteenth century, those parts of the performance should be done as they would have experienced it with just candlelight in otherwise total darkness. It was relatively easy to black out all natural light but less simple to provide the right lighting effect. Before the mind-boggling Health and Safety Regulations which now seem at times to be in place to restrict initiative, theatrical enthusiasm swept us on. Then one day only shortly before the sold out opening night we had a visit from the Station Officer for the Fire Prevention Department of the South Yorkshire County Fire Service. John Bostwick's memory of the visit remains quite clearly with him to the present day!

'One day in 1986 an application appeared on my desk for an Occcasional Stage Play Licence signed by M D Dyke from The Oaks School which was in my area so as Station Officer I carried out an inspection.

I met Mrs Dyke at the school whereupon she informed me that the production was called, *Children of the Dark*. I asked if any flames or pyrotechnics were to be involved. She replied that there would be as at one point in the play the lights would be dimmed and the children would be holding lighted candles. After she picked me up from the floor, I explained to her the dangers of hot wax dripping on to the children's hands which could cause them to drop the lighted candles with obvious consequences.

By the look on her face I could see that she was very disappointed to say the least. I had to think very quickly on my feet to come up with an alternative idea and said that if every child held a baked bean tin half filled with sand, with a small candle half buried in the sand, that I would accept that. Mel was delighted and accepted my compromise. The play went ahead with great success and I have been a friend of Mel Dyke ever since.'

Heavy sighs of relief followed that visit as we realised what at catastrophe it could have been if we had been visited by anyone with a 'jobsworth' frame of mind!

He has been a friend too; often through his other commitments all linked to bettering the development and promotion of the town. For many years Chair of Holgate School's governing body he and his wife, Kathy, went above and beyond the call of duty, not simply attending all events but actually doing the cooking for some of them. His support of Dr John Foster's efforts to recognise the work of James Hudson Taylor in spreading Christianity across China was seminal in engaging Barnsley Civic Trust to provide two blue plaques on the site of Taylor's birthplace in the centre of Barnsley, one in English and one in Mandarin, which already attract overseas visitors to the town. His latest educational venture is to raise a similar profile of another son of the town, John Hugh Burland, whose part in the Chartist Movement and his *Annals of Barnsley* remain an influential reference point for many of the most prominent historians of the period.

Barnsley's public recognition of the missionary work of James Hudson Taylor in China.

It was predictable that the heavily-based mining community would attend the event, but we were really unprepared for the depth of appreciation and heights of response. Following John Bostwick's spontaneous support others were equally generous with their praise. Lord and Lady Mason accepted an invitation to attend becoming so engaged with the performance that they have remained amongst the most stalwart and loyal supporters throughout all subsequent productions. Dr Mary Jefferson, a highly valued Senior Education Adviser with Barnsley MBC, who had seen the Darton production led the wonderful Rev Derek Birch, incumbent of Silkstone's Parish Church, to us. He not only advised and helped with our research, allowed us to display the original church Burial Register and attended the performances, but immediately spotted the potential for the inclusion of the play in the impending two years later 150th Anniversary of the Huskar Tragedy,

Jack Wood of Silkstone and Dodworth miner Tommy Wadsworth also attended the Oaks memorial performance and wept. Derek Birch was already ahead of them but they made the first informal approach and were instrumental in the school agreeing to repeat the performance. It would be in the old church of All Saints and St James the Compassionate beside the memorial to the twenty-six children and on 4 July 1988, the 150th Anniversary of the tragedy.

Active local historian Jack Wood's booklet on the tragedy continued to widen knowledge and stimulate awareness in the school. Through Tommy Wadsworth's fascinating collection of mining memorabilia I found my own father's pit checks, which his great grandchildren now have, and many other families were similarly able to trace their history. With the typical three degrees of separation in Barnsley, we found that Tommy's son was a member of the same band as Terry Mullen. Milestones, another folk band was made up of five local teachers: Terry, Ed Gabbani, Les Foweather, Tony McNally and Mick Wadsworth. The Wadsworths are a typical mining family of the era, father in it all his life, body and soul; son educationally enabled to make choices. Mick's first choice was sport, particularly football and his talent in that has taken him far and world wide. A Diploma in PE backed up by a Postgraduate Certificate in Education from Sheffield University in Maths and PE led to teaching first in local schools then regional youth coaching before five years as England National Youth Coach and a scout for Bobby Robson's England team. Predictably Barnsley FC would be his choice to move with the big boys into coaching and then managing teams from Barnsley FC to Carlisle, Norwich, Scarborough Southampton, Oldham and Huddersfield before via the Congo to manage the Portuguese Super League team Bierra Mar. But from the reciprocal affection with which he speaks of him, I would gamble that his favourite time ever was the two years he spent at Newcastle, as Head Coach and Assistant to the late, great Sir Bobby Robson.

But his favourite memento, that which he values most is not from the many trophies, titles and medals Mick Wadsworth has collected in his own impressive career. No flash gold medallion; what he proudly keeps closest to his heart is a plain gold chain on which hang two of the pit checks his own father wore underground during his lifetime as a miner.

Mick Wadsworth proudly wearing his father's pit checks.

I had never realised how personally significant 1986, the 50th anniversary of the 1936 Carlton Pit Disaster was for me personally. I had been aware that my own father and his brothers had been involved in the rescue work on the shift following the explosion at that pit, which happened before I was born. My elder cousin Iris recalls her mother's account of her father, Charlie Robinson, who was on 'regular days' that week coming home from work. 'He looked terrible when he walked through the door and when my mother asked what was wrong all he could say was, "We've been picking bones and bodies up all shift". His dinner was ready, but he couldn't even look at it. He was sick and could only drink some cold water, then went straight up to bed. He couldn't face going back to that pit for a week and after that if he ever had 'monk on'* we'd know why.'

My own dad never spoke to me of that day in his lifetime. It was my mother who told me much later of the nightmares my dad had suffered

---

* Used in local dialect to describe someone who is being uncommunicative: 'having the monk on' is taken to be a reference to the monks at nearby Monk Bretton Priory, observing the silence of their Cluniac Order.

from that day for the rest of his life. It was not however until I saw his photograph in Brian Elliott's book *South Yorkshire Mining Disasters,* Volume 2, that I fully understood the trauma.

English teacher Janet Richardson, who drawn by the experience of appearing in the production of *Children of the Dark*, later looked more deeply into the background of the victims, and found a link to her own family history.

'As I was brought up in Silkstone Common I had always known something of the story of the children who were drowned in the flood. I can even remember my mum showing me the actual 'dayhole' in Knabbs Wood where the tragedy took place. Therefore I was very keen to be involved in the production of *Children of the Dark*

August 1936, tragedy at Carlton pit. Photograph by kind permission of the *Barnsley Chronicle.*

while I was teaching at The Oaks School in the 1980s. However it is only more recently that I have discovered that my mother's family had a connection to one of the children who died in the tragedy.

Sarah Newton, at eight years old, was one of the youngest children to die in Huskar Pit. Her mother was Ann Newton who became a widow in 1851 when her husband was killed in an accident, leaving her with eight children, the youngest less than a year old.

Ann (43) remarried in 1852 and this is where the Horsfield connection comes in. Charles Horsfield (55) was a widower with five children, the youngest being ten years old. Two years later Ann and Charles had a boy, James Horsfield, who would have been half brother of Sarah, who died sixteen years previously. James Horsfield was their only child as Charles died a year later leaving Ann a widow for the second time in four years, with even more children to care for. It is James Horsfield who I find was my grandad's father and my great-grandad.

The 1861 census shows that six-year-old James was living with his mother and three of Ann's children from her first marriage. James is listed as a scholar, but his half-brother Joseph Newton, ten years old is a colliery labourer.

The 1871 census shows that James, aged sixteen, is still living at home and working as a carter. Ann, aged sixty-one, was working as a greengrocer. Most of the young men of James' age are working underground so, despite her difficult circumstances, Ann managed to keep her youngest son from working down the pit.

Ann must have been a remarkable woman. She brought up her own children, probably some of her stepchildren, as well as the child he'd had at the age of forty-five and it appears that she also worked as a greengrocer. She died in her seventies.

It came as something of a shock to find about Sarah Newton and our family's link to her, but would guess that most of the families who were living in Silkstone at the time would have had connections to these children.'

Mike Swallow's account:

'The atmosphere in Silkstone Church that afternoon on 4 July 1988 was unbelievable. At times you could hear the silence; you could almost smell the fear and torment of all those young souls who were trapped in the swirling waters of the living hell hole at Huskar Pit one hundred and fifty years ago. Man appears to be driven by material gain, the more he gets, the more he wants. The United Kingdom has made huge strides towards the protection of children. However, the exploitation of children is still paramount in the sweat shops in other parts of the world.

The 1838 tragedy which touched the nation's heart brought a Royal Commission of Enquiry and lead to the Mines Act 1842 which banned women and girls from employment and outlawed the employment of boys under the age of ten. (The Abolition of Slavery Act was introduced five years earlier in 1833!) Very gradual improvements were introduced; seventy years after the Huskar Disaster:

The Coal Mines Regulations Act (1908)
Employment of Young Persons and Childrens Act 1920
Children and Young Persons Act 1933
Factories Act 1937
Education Act 1944

It has taken a century towards obtaining justice and well being for our children. WHY?

This was the result of a wonderful job done well and indicated hard work in both education and pursuit in the welfare of children. It was a truly unforgettable evening.'

Stan and Connie Barstow also attended that 150th anniversary service at which Stan stated publicly that he had never in his life been more moved by a church service. It was not only the wonderful range of talent and control of the children's young voices in their roles as the children whose bodies lay outside the church, but once again the power of the music provided by Dick Walker and Off the Cuff. The haunting voice of Betty Martin echoed round a church converted by a cascade of white flowers from ceiling to floor depicting the scene when the deluge of water caused the deaths of twenty-six children with an average age of eleven working as miners. Twenty-six individual flower arrangements each named for one of the victims were also created by the ladies of Worsborough Flower Club who, working together for days, reconstructed the scene creating an unforgettable visual impact.

Connie and Stan Barstow with Dick Walker and a cast member. Photograph by kind permission of Mike Swallow.

Taken in a relaxing moment during rehearsals. The performance itself though was unsmiling. Photograph by kind permission of Mike Swallow.

The Archbishop of York, David Hope, took part of the service.

The television coverage of these events brought the school to the attention of a BBC team looking for a school in which to film John Godber's production of his newest work, *My Kingdom for a Horse*. Funding, facilities, materials and specialism support within the film crew

The procession into Silkstone Church: Rev Derek Birch is third from the right. Photograph by kind permission of Mike Swallow.

The Archbishop of York leads the 150th Anniversary service in 1988. Photograph by kind permission of Mike Swallow.

for acting, producing and directing, and also in technology, lighting, sound set and scenery with hitherto undreamed of opportunities for children across the Arts came with bonuses across the curriculum and the school. Celebrated author John Godber taught some English groups, six children were given contracts for acting roles, and examination groups in the Art Department were able to become engaged in work to provide scenery for the film and in doing so had unique portfolio opportunities and higher grades. Every child in school was seen on film – and all in a day's work, to accommodate filming, I had to share my office with a young actor named Sean Bean...

The Oaks – Interviews and life stories for the Bus to Barnsley Market.

When *Look North* featured the production, Mike McCarthy who had reported on the Silkstone and John Godber's work in the school, then followed up filming the group in the first underground visit by a group of school children to the National Coal Mining Museum. The English Department's new technology was quickly put to use in children writing up their experiences of the visit as part of their school work

Shortly after which, approached by Yorkshire Arts Circus to become involved in a community book project, children were engaged in writing and comparing their own life stories with visitors including some of the older local residents from the earlier Zen garden project. Supervised here by one of the best English teachers I have ever known, John Lomas, their reactions and those of the visitors when they received typed up and printed copies of their individual inputs at the end of the day, from the children, were a delight to see.

*Mike McCarthy,
representing* Look North,
*was a frequent visitor to
Barnsley during the 1980s.*
Photo by kind permission of Mike McCarthy.

Chapter 3

The 1984-85 Miners' Strike

'The 1984–85 miners' strike stands as one of those rare events when those living through it just knew they were witnessing a major social, political and economic event. To put it quite simply, Britain would never be the same again.

Whole communities, in most cases located in rural areas with very little economic infrastructure, lost their *raison d'etre*. Whole families, extended families even, lost their livelihoods and their pride. And the Thatcher government got what it wanted; the defeat of a union which had been a thorn in the side of the Tory party for many years and a significant breakthrough in terms of establishing the free-market, *laissez-faire* economy that was the dream of the new Right. What followed was the rapid consolidation of a new structure for the UK economy built not on One Nation principle, but on free market principles, driven by what was to prove to be an ultimately unsustainable financial services sector.

Never mind the massive contraction in the coal industry and the 'dash for gas', which would in the future see the UK become dangerously dependent on foreign energy sources. Never mind the social costs and the welfare costs of wholesale industrial contraction, costs that remain with us today as we struggle to deal with the long-term and inter-generational unemployment that grew out of this shrinking of the economies of Wales and Scotland, and of the English regions. Never mind the fact that along with the savage job losses in industries such as coal went the workforce skills built up over generations of manufacturing in places such as Sheffield and Barnsley. All that mattered was the ideology of the market and the ability of the sharp-suited tenants of the City to turn over a quick profit.

No wonder we all remember the miners' strike.

But we remember it too because of the heartache it caused. I remember visiting a family in Rotherham, half way through the strike, just before the winter was setting in. My mum's cousin worked at Silverwood and made it clear as I walked through the door, please, no talk about the strike. Even then the strain was beginning to show, amongst workers determined to stay loyal to their union and its campaign but who nevertheless felt the frustration and the pain of being out of work for so long.

I remember the police officers, bussed in from other police forces and transported in convoys to places of safety once off duty. Some would boast of their overtime earnings, a poor boast

Angela Smith MP for Penistone and Stocksbridge. Photograph by kind permission of Angela Smith MP.

in bad taste, given the enormity of what was at stake for those who were, after all, only fighting for the right to work.

We remember too the spirit of those who supported the miners, families, friends and activists from across the country. It was a support network which reasserted itself in 1992, when there was a massive, popular backlash against a further, huge round of pit closures and when even the workers in Kensington department stores leaned out of windows to support those of us marching in support of pit communities up and down the country.

More than anything, though, I remember the aftermath. The chronic unemployment and despair in communities across South Yorkshire, the slag heaps and waste reminding us all of what had been. The call centres going up and the development of the Cortonwood retail centre, on the site of the pit where the strike had started. I remember a pub in a village nearby, where a new landlord tried to put up a portrait of a local lad who had become a major Tory politician – William Hague. Only they had to take it down again pretty smartish, on pain of losing their loyal custom.

Now, over twenty years on, it's hard to find reminders of our coal heritage in South Yorkshire. It's almost as though someone, somewhere, was determined to wipe out any witness to the industry that sustained our area for so many decades, so many centuries. But folks' memories are still strong and that is the route to what would be the most enduring and important tribute of all to King Coal; the recording of the voices of those who worked in the industry, for the sake of our future, as well our past.'

Angela Smith, MP for Penistone and Stocksbridge

Angela Smith MP for Penistone and Stocksbridge is absolutely right. In 1992 the greatest fear was that the closures would automatically bring a return to unemployment and to the financial hardship of 1984–85.

Glen Cook was a miner at that time:

'I don't know if you were involved in the 1984 miners' strike yourself or have an interest in that period. Maybe you were involved or possibly you could be looking for stories that may help you understand what the whole episode was all about. My story revolves around a time some three months after the start of the strike on the 31st May 1984 with my wife, my niece and her husband at Skirlington on the east coast just north of Hornsea. My brother and his wife had a caravan there and the four of us went there for a few days free holiday. My niece's husband, Steve, was also on strike and so a free holiday was all we could afford.

Dad's health had been failing for quite a while prior to the trip and I hadn't been able to see as much of him over the last few weeks as I had sold my car. The maintenance was too much as there was no income at all in my household and we had even had to stop paying the mortgage like most other families. Regardless of this we were having a reasonably good time going for walks on the beach and around Bridlington although I do remember there was a biting wind even at that time of year, but we had left Grimethorpe and Barrow collieries well behind for now.

We were all in the caravan on the second afternoon settled down with a cup of tea when there was a knock on the caravan door. It was the site manager who had received a telephone call from my brother saying we should go home. We immediately packed everything up and jumped into our Debbie's little red Mini 850. Debbie's driving was reminiscent of the old RAC rally drivers but she did an excellent job considering she was eight months pregnant at the time. We went straight to Barnsley District General and when they eventually let me into the ward dad was lying in bed with oxygen pipes attached to his nose and mouth. He was a fairly tall chap my dad with a really good head of hair. His physique was also quite impressive but was a man of few words. My four foot eleven mother ruled the roost at our house.

He drifted in and out of sleep and my brother, John, was already there with him. We stayed until it was the end of the visiting hours and before we left we leant over his bed to say goodbye to him. He managed to speak but we couldn't make out what he said. We leaned nearer to him.

"What's that dad" asked our John.

"You're a pair of grand lads" he managed to say again and then closed his eyes.

We went round to our Barry's, my other brother and the eldest of the three of us and. and

I said I would go back to the hospital that night with our Barry. I think I felt a bit guilty having been away for the last couple of days but wanted to be next to dad anyway. When the two of us arrived that evening dad had been moved to a side room by himself. As we walked in the room I saw him lying in the bed, again with oxygen pipes attached to him and other monitoring devices for his heartbeat and blood pressure etc. He was sleeping constantly now and we stayed with him well into the night. Barry went into a side room designated for visitors and caught up with some sleep while I stayed with dad. I could see dad's breathing was getting shallower but I kept talking to him hoping I get would some sort of response.

Eventually a doctor came in to do some tests and so I went off to the side room and sat with our Barry for a couple of minutes. We then went back to dad's room where the doctor was still carrying out tests and informed us it was not looking good. "Come on dad" urged Barry, like me hoping he would get some response. The doctor asked us to leave and after a few minutes, which seemed like an age, he came out and told us dad had passed away.

After the formalities we went back to our Barry's house and broke the news to mum. We all stayed there that night and the next morning I went for a walk in Locke Park with my wife where the anger inside me grew and grew. Angry because I hadn't been able to see as much of dad as I had done before the start of the strike. Angry because I had to sell my car and couldn't get over to see him as I used to call in every day either on my way to work or on my way home from work. Angry because I couldn't afford the bus fare more than once a week.

Although I felt the strike was for all the right reasons it really rankled with me, like a festering sore that other people had determined my destiny, which I didn't realise at the time, for the next twelve months. I decided at that point that I was going to get a job which meant that I decided when I was going to work and when I didn't want to go to work. After returning to work there was a definite change in atmosphere and I think some of the soul of the place had left us. It didn't stop us knuckling down and getting on with the job as we had always done though and slowly things did get back to some kind of normality.

I made a determined effort after the end of the strike to get myself another job and applied for many jobs over the coming years, about fifty, and got a few interviews without success but I kept plugging away. Finally, in 1988, I was offered four jobs more or less at the same time. That does wonders for your ego.

I finally opted for one as service engineer with a premier brand and started work on 3 January 1989 after taking voluntary redundancy as well. It really was a lovely job and a total contrast to working at Grimethorpe Colliery. I was now working in people's houses, going on my first helicopter ride to a gas rig out in the North Sea, another first, and meeting people like Rowan Atkinson, The Duchess of Norfolk and the Countess of Arundel. After two and a half years they made me a senior engineer and then another two and a half years later they made me the service manager for the north of England, North Wales and Scotland.

I was now involved in service strategies and influencing the direction of the service department and I loved every minute of it. I spent a vast majority of time in the head office in Abingdon near Oxford and worked with a multitude of lovely colleagues. All my sporting activities took place with them such as badminton, squash twice a week and five a side football. Oh and the pub quiz every Thursday night in a pub at the side of the Thames. This is where the similarity was with the mining community. We worked together and we socialised together and so in that respect nothing had changed but in actual fact everything had changed.

I remember dad once saying to me,

"Study at technical college and you might get to be a foreman like our Barry and John". Well, I didn't quite make a foreman at the pit but I still think dad would have been quite proud of me.'

The year-long strike had not been simply about a political principle, for communities which believed they were fighting for their traditional way of life it was much more than that. In a long and demanding year some men felt they lost far more than a year's earnings, they also lost their traditional place as head of the family, the rightful main 'provider' for 'the wife and kids'. For some of them the relationships were unable to survive that perceived degradation. For others the shared struggle strengthened marriages and friendships, forging bonds that could never be broken. In 2012 Ann Dooley recalls her memories of those days for me with a rueful smile and stories that simultaneously brought tears and smiles.

'I had just had my youngest and after the birth the midwife asked me if we were alright for coal at home. She must have known what she was saying to me because when I said that we were very low on it when I went into hospital she added that of course a Health Visitor would have to check that the house would be warm enough for a new baby to go to before they would be allowed to go home. I was really upset, missing the other children if I had to stay in too, wondering how I would get to the hospital in Barnsley to visit if not, and knowing our coal situation wasn't likely to be getting any better.

Dennis got in touch with the Union who said in the circumstances they would do what they could, but before they could do anything word must have got round in the village. Neighbours, friends and even people we hardly knew turned up at the house, every one of them carrying a bucketful of coal, or whatever they could spare. So when they did arrive to check our coal bunker it was full to the top and I was allowed to go home straight away – and take the baby with me. Some of the people who did that were so short of coal themselves that they had to come back a day or two later and take some back. It's rare to find the sort of shared community spirit and generosity we had in those days, the old older folk used to say that's how it was in the war; it certainly kept us going.'

That aspect reminds me still of a young French Assistant at Darton High School in the 1970s, who after making his first underground visit to a coal mine with us came out of Woolley Colliery saying, "I am a Frenchman, we know about Liberty and Equality, but only today I have really understood the meaning of Fraternity."

'Dennis and Shaun went with the others riddling coal or chopping logs for fuel, and I only found out years later that he had another arrangement with Shaun. If he was out when the post came, a brown envelope would most likely be a bill; so Shaun was to keep that one safe and give it to Dennis when he got back home.

The Union helped with vouchers and whilst nobody wanted to take their children to the store set up as a centre for the scheme of aid children's clothing or to go to the soup kitchens, we knew that everybody who did go now was in the same position as us. The ladies who provided and cooked the food at the soup kitchen in Shafton were sensitive to that and they were so nice, you didn't really feel quite so bad. It bothered the kids though, didn't matter how we tried to put it to them they were not used to charity and they hated it.'

Others' views varied judging by these accounts from pupils at the time.

'When the strike began it meant I had to put up with my dad being at home all day. He just used to sit there with his feet up doing nothing. I couldn't stop in the house and look at his face.

Oh, yes! I remember it well, all the hardship my friends, the community and the whole country suffered and the relief that followed when it was finally over. The news flash at the end of it, after nearly a whole year! No-one uninvolved can imagine the hardship these people went through.

It was enough having the miners out on strike, but there was violence too. Men had been killed, a taxi driver, whose wife had just given birth to a baby, was killed while taking some scabs to work. A concrete slab was thrown off a bridge and went through the windscreen of the car. David Jones was killed on a picket line.

Arthur Scargill said that the Government would close a lot of pits in the near future. This was reviled. He also said they would privatise pits in the future and this also was reviled.

It was a school morning we heard about the miners' strike. The class was in physical science doing an experiment outside with thermometers to see how cold it was. We heard a lot of shouting at the pit and saw many police officers. The class asked the teacher what it was all about and he told us it was a strike.

Not long after Christmas my dad came home and told us that one of my uncles had been taken to jail for swearing at a police officer. The police had punched him and given him a black eye. He was in there a week.

When we arrived people were already there raging in anger when the first set of scabs arrived. Suddenly an array of different coloured horses came over the hill. When the horses got down to us we started moving slowly backwards out of the way of these massive four legged animals. Everyone was pushing and I was moving slowly towards the back to save my ribs. The police got one of my dad's mates and searched his body and his wax coat. They found a knife, which he always carried with him, but they knew that this could be used as a weapon. They bundled him into the back of a big van and kicked and punched him.

The cops advanced over the horizon. Their helmets glistening in the eerie sun glow. Disciplined, all in formation, quite unlike the miners. The miners were rowdy, shouting abuse at the cops and soon the clash would come.

It was a time when we had to go without or cut down on the things we would normally have such as best steak or worrying about having the television on at any time of the day without worrying whether you could pay the bill.

The police were soon brought in to deal with the miners. Riot gear was brought out and the fight to stop them began. Every day innocent men and women would be admitted to hospital just because they happened to be passing by.

As the winter months approached I was sent to the YPO (grov shop) for shoes and a duffel coat. The shoes were really awful but we had no alternatives.

I looked at the clock and it was half past seven so I got dressed. I pulled on my worn blue uniform thinking of how embarrassed I felt the first day I went to school in school shop clothes. As I went downstairs I could hear my mother and realised this was the first time I had ever heard my Mam cry.

It started four days before my birthday; because of it quiet family men would end up in jail and fight or shout insults at people they had known for the best part of their life. Families would be split apart with a hatchet of bitterness that only time could heal – no, it wasn't a civil war, just an ordinary industrial dispute that lasted for almost a year. My dad had no option but to go on strike. His pit was already due for closure. Not going on strike would have meant certain closure. He was not a staunch militant, but someone trying to get compensation for a disability resulting from an accident down the pit.

Everybody at some point had to visit the dreaded school shop. I remember it well. A wrinkled old lady placed the coats in front of us and I couldn't believe my eyes – a brown duffel coat with large chocolate brown toggles "Oh no Mam, I can't wear that". The shoes were black. They didn't fit me and to this very day I have scars on both heels to remind me how small they were.

It was four years ago and a little too hard for me to understand then but its scars will remain forever. Picket lines, a mass of yellow tipped with black and navy and armed with shields and truncheons. Hundreds of police mostly southern b******s as my dad called them and the rest either soldiers in disguise or a few local Bobbies.

The strike made the community strong and I'll never forget the chants and the songs. My family lived on £16.24 a week for a year so my dad and his mates could fight not just for their jobs but for the country as well. Now the police hold community talks with false smiles and promises. But they will never gain my respect and, in my opinion, this Government is the root of this evil.'

Shaun's own contemporary account is comprehensively clear:

The Strike

'In 1974 a man called Arthur Scargill said to the miners 'hundreds of pits will all be closed and thousands of people will lose their jobs'. Nobody believed him, the miners didn't believe him and the press ridiculed him. This split the NUM It was 1984 when a pit called Cortonwood came out on strike. This was the first pit to come out on strike. About a month later, other pits came out in support of Cortonwood, such as Grimethorpe. It had taken the NUM ten years to realise what Arthur Scargill had said was true. The time had eventually come which Arthur Scargill had predicted. It was the miners versus the Government.

It was a cold Sunday morning when me and my dad set off to go coal picking. We took a shovel, a sieve and a couple of coal sacks. My dad shovelled up a mixture of coal, coal dust and dirt, he then put it in my sieve, which I shook until there was only coal left. I poured the coal into the sack. After a while, I got pretty bored of this and decided that I would go exploring. The reason I went away from the place, was not only because I was bored, but because I was scared that someone may recognise me and tell my friends. Then I heard a distant voice calling my name, I instantly knew that it was my dad's voice, so I casually strolled towards his, hoping that we would be going home, my prayers were answered. We got in the car and set off home. When we got home my mum told us that we were going to a party for our dinner. It wasn't a bit like a party, in fact it was more like a funeral. There were people of all shapes and sizes, all in this one big hall. As we were eating our dinner, I heard my mum say to my dad, 'I hate these damn soup kitchens'. I hadn't realised this was a soup kitchen, and I felt very degraded. I suddenly realised how desperate our situation was. The next few days went alright until Wednesday afternoon, when a Wigfalls van pulled up outside our house. A tall man got out of the van and walked down our path. I could tell by the expression on my mum's face that he wasn't the bearer of good news. My dad took the man into another room, and two minutes later came out and walked towards the TV set. I watched my dad pull out the leads from the back of the TV and video with a defeated look on his face. I scowled at the man, wishing I was ten years older so that I could throw him out of our house. He picked up our video, and walking out of our house, I could see the grin on his face. This was quite a shock, but when he came back and took the TV, my heart sank into an endless pit. However, I didn't show this, because I knew that if I got upset, so would my sister. The next day we went blackberry picking, so that my dad could make some wine. I think this was because we couldn't afford to buy it, but there isn't many things you can afford, living on thirty pounds a week with three kids, is there?

The next few months passed ordinary. The month leading up to Christmas was packed with my mum telling us that we wouldn't get much for Christmas. On Christmas Eve, we went up to the soup kitchen because they were giving presents to the kids. This was the last place I wanted to go on Christmas Eve. But I could not say anything, because my sister was very excited about it. To go back to school we had to go to the school shop to get free school uniforms. When I went back to school I had to have free meals which was very embarrassing. The only way we could go on holiday was to borrow a friend's caravan. There were four adults and five kids, and it was great fun. A couple of weeks later came one of the happiest days in our life, it was around one o'clock on the 3 March when the strike finished. All my aunties and uncles came up to our house crying with relief. I walked into my bedroom and fell on my knees thanking God that it was all over. Later on that day, the miners of Grimethorpe pit marched back to work, led by my great uncle Cliff. Even though it was a hard fight, it was a just fight, and one that is not over yet. Privatisation is the next battle.' *Shaun Dooley*

Ann Dooley continues:

'Christmas loomed with very little prospect of presents for anybody but then surprise gifts arrived from the Russian miners who sent a present for every single child in a mining family. Shaun got a remote controlled car, Stephanie a doll and there was even a Teddy for the baby Kimberley. We had great help from the family, my Mum and Dad bought us a pram and a cot and each week they brought us a basics food parcel; butter, flour, sugar, milk, bread, vegetables, a tin of meat etc, and every week without fail there would be a large tin of salmon in it. We called it our Red Cross parcel and were so grateful for it then but I can't see a tin of salmon now without thinking about those days! Sunday dinners were out of the question so, like most people, we went back to our parents and shared their Sunday roast.

It was a massive blow when the rented TV had to go, we got a little portable one that the whole family could sit round and watch, but it was another shame you felt. We'd never had debts and Dennis was worried about me worrying, he knew how much it would upset me to know if we were to start now. I was terrified we would lose everything; I can remember crying that the house would have to go and we would have to move and rent somewhere else. But bleak though they were these were also the days when things were done on a personal basis at your local bank. Abbey National froze our mortgage for twelve months in arrears and then simply restarted it after the strike. I don't think it would happen these days!

Shaun Dooley and Simon Hirst at Barnsley College Open Day in 2012. Photograph by kind permission of Barnsley College.

It's difficult for anybody who wasn't there to understand because they were really hard times but ironically we have some really happy memories and we made new friends too. Since nobody could afford to go out to the pub or the club we'd pick blackberries and other wild ingredients and everyone made their own home brew. Then we thought we'd start a monthly wine tasting club at each others' homes which was a real laugh. Considered assessments of the efforts on the tasting group results brought comments ranging from, 'Not bad this!' to 'What the Hell's in this?' But we still drank it!"

When the strike ended in tears, and Cliff Sellars led the march back to work we realised that we could put the new found unity of purpose to other good effect. There was no youth or community centre in Shafton so we set about to get one. We leafleted the area and as I was a trained Youth Worker with an amateur dramatics song and dance background, I started to produce shows to raise funds. We did Cinderella with Shaun's first big role as Buttons, I was Cinders, Dennis was a Henchman, Stephanie was a fairy and even the baby, Kim, was included as a very small fairy! The final result was a true Community Centre – one built by a community for a community. A threat that could have destroyed that very community and was also the start of my own children's now very successful lives in theatre and film; I can look back and say that the ill wind did blow in some good changes too.'

When Shaun Dooley and Simon Hirst readily agreed to return to their old Sixth Form College for the official Open Day at Barnsley College for the re-opening after rebuild in 2012, this time it was as celebrity guests and in real Grimethorpe style for a balloon launch.

That day Head of PR and Communications Mel Jenkinson greeted us with the information that she already knew Shaun from school in Grimethorpe. He recognised her instantly and their way back when chat revealed that just as Shaun's was, her initial interest in writing was nurtured there. Then they are off, giggling and testing each other's memories. Her opening comment struck a cord with me leading me to go back through the children's writing which Max Bristowe had so carefully preserved. And sure enough Melanie Jenkinson's work was there – but although written in the first person singular, this was not a personal record of what had happened in her home or family. Her father was a glassworker not a miner and her work was instead a clear indication of her ability to record creatively mature and perceptive observations of what was happening to others around her, including her friends.

'When I returned home from school my mother was in the kitchen unpacking the shopping.

"Had a nice day love?" she asked.

"Not bad", I replied, hanging up my jacket.

I stared at the items on the table – one tin of beans, two tins of soup, a loaf of white bread and a block of margarine. Even though we still had a few things left over from last week, because mum was far too upset about the strike that she hadn't been eating, the shopping that she had bought today was only a meagre amount of what we usually had.

We were only six weeks in to the strike and already suffering from the effects of no wages coming in. I went into the living-room and switched on the television, news about the strike was on, so I quickly turned it over to watch Grange Hill, because I knew mum wouldn't let me watch it if she knew the strike was on the other side.

"Where's dad?" I shouted to mum.

"He's gone picketing", she replied.

"Has he gone with Susan's dad?"

"I don't know, why?"

"Nothing, I just wondered, that's all."

Susan was my best friend, and she wanted me to go round to their house that evening, but I didn't like going round when her dad was in, because he was always in a bad mood. I was sat in my bedroom doing my homework, when I heard the back door slam. I knew it was dad returning from a day on the picket line, then I heard my mother shout me for my dinner. I went downstairs, and sat at the table listening to my dad telling us about his day. When I had finished my soup, I went over to Susan's house to listen to her records.

As months went by, everyday things became worse. We had to stop the papers and milk, and the telephone was disconnected because we were unable to pay the bills.

"We'll just have to manage" is what my mother would say.

Saturday is the best day of the week for me, because I spend the whole day at my grandma's while dad goes picketing, and mum goes to try and find work. My grandma has started to give me a little extra pocket money now, as my mum and dad can't afford it. What little money we do have, has got to be saved for essential things, such as food and paying the bills.

I saw Susan in the street, and she asked me if I wanted to go to the jumble sale which was being held in the school hall.

"I'll have to ask first", I told her and went inside. My grandma was sat in the chair knitting a blue pullover for my mother.

"Can I go to the jumble sale?" I asked her.

"Off course you can", she replied. "Go fetch my purse." I ran into the kitchen and reached for the brown leather purse from out of the drawer, then I took it back into the room. My grandma opened it, and took three pounds out, which she gave to me.

"Now don't lose it", she said, "And watch the road." I gave her a quick kiss on the cheek and ran to meet Susan who was waiting at the corner of the street. Inside the school hall everyone was shoving and pushing trying to find the best bargains.

There were clothes, toys, books and bric-a-brac stalls. Mr Charlesworth was trying to encourage people to buy tickets for his raffle, which was in aid of the church. I had two goes in the lucky dip. The first time I got a bag of sweets, and the second a pack of pens. I bought a *Jackie* annual and a little pot jug decorated with delicate pink roses for my grandma.

When I returned home that evening there seemed to be a strange atmosphere in the house. Dad was sat in the chair watching the news, whilst my mum was making a cup of tea in the kitchen.

"I've been to a jumble sale at school today, with Susan." I told my dad, trying to break the silence.

"I don't want you associating with that girl anymore", he said.

"Why?" I asked, not quite sure of what he was trying to tell me.

"Because her dad's a b...... scab that's why, and I don't want any daughter of mine mixing with that sort."

"But she's my best friend."

"I don't care if she's the Queen of England, you'll do as I say. We are having to manage, and they should do the same. There's some men on that picket line without a penny, and five kids to look after. We've all got to pull together if we want to win this strike, and we'll never do that if there's folk like him going back to work. We've got to fight for our right."

"It's not her fault her dad's gone back to work, and you can't stop me from seeing her."

He jumped up out of the chair and came towards me raising his hand shouting,

"You're getting two big for your boots young lady. When I tell you to do something, you'll do it."

"Shut up." I yelled back at him and ran out of the room slamming the door behind me.

My mother came to wake me earlier than usual this morning.

"Come on, get up, we're going to get you some new clothes today", she said, opening the curtains. Without further questions, I got dressed and went downstairs for my breakfast. Dad had already gone picketing, and I was glad because I didn't want to face him after last night's argument. I was surprised that mum didn't mention anything about it either.

In the town my mum knew exactly where we were going, and I felt rather happy about going for a new school uniform, until we reached the shop that is.

"Come on, love", she said.

"I'm not, definitely not, going in there", I protested.

"Why ever not?"

"Because it's a right grave shop, that's why."

She grabbed hold of my arm and dragged me inside. I could feel everyone staring at me as my mother held up awful jumpers and blouses against me, and then, if that wasn't humiliating enough, we went upstairs looking for a pair of shoes and trainers.

I was so relieved when we were stood in the bus queue waiting to go home.

"I am not wearing any of that, I can tell you now", I told her pointing to the bag.

"Look, young lady," she said, "You will wear these things whether you like them or not", waving the plastic carriers with 'Charity Shop' wrote all over it, in my face. "Your dad's on strike and we can't afford to buy you a new school uniform. The money we do have is to buy food and the bills and when shops are giving away perfectly decent clothes like these, it's an offer we just can't refuse especially in the situation we're in."

We travelled the rest of the way home in silence. When we reached our house, Mrs Brown, our next door neighbour was stood at the back door waiting for us.

"Is something wrong?" my mother asked.

"I think it would be better if we go inside," replied Mrs Brown.

"Why, what's the matter?" my mother questioned whilst unlocking the door.

When we were sat down in the living room, Mrs Brown continued.

"I'm afraid your husband has been sent to jail for attacking a police officer on the picket line. He should be home in a couple of days, but nothings certain just yet", she told us.

Mum and I sat on the settee staring at each other. "Well, we'll just have to manage," my mother said.

For another girl it was not a story she made up. It tells how she lived through it first hand.

'That night it was on *Calendar* and my mum and dad were talking about it a lot. We didn't think much about it but at school everyone was talking about the strike because everyone's dad was involved. Even the teachers asked about it. A few days passed and we lost interest, we just got used to it. Then a few weeks passed and they were still on strike. It was when I thought we'd starve to death I began to take notice. I started to ask questions and I think they got fed up of me asking so mum sat me down and we had a talk about everything. About how we'd have to cut down on things and not ask for things we knew we couldn't have. She told me it was hard on them too, that we'd all have to stick together and help each other whenever we could. She's good my mum, she was very practical about everything but not harsh or cold and I began to understand things I hadn't understood before like why my dad went to the soup kitchen for his dinner. Why my grandad had been sending my uncle over to our house with food, meat and fresh vegetables. I'd hear them arguing because she wouldn't take money off him that is why he sent food, she wouldn't let good food go to waste and he knew that. I think it was harder on my mum as she's very proud and hated the thought of accepting any sort of charity. I knew we'd hardly any money but when my dad told me I was going to the school shop I nearly died. I'd always thought the school shop was for very poor people. My dad said everyone was going to the school shop. I tried not to look upset because that would only make him feel worse about not having money to buy us things. I hated money, it was because of money all this was happening and my dad was on strike and upset. The day of the dreaded school shop arrived and I hoped I'd get some of those nice black shoes with the blue stripe and the bow on the front, everyone was wearing those. A lady came through the door with a sheet and shouted my name and we followed her through the door. She asked me what size I took, and I saw them horrible brown shoes with a silver buckle. I prayed they wouldn't fit me. Just my luck they were my size and I didn't even glimpse a pair of black shoes!

My mum always woke me for school so I knew something was wrong. She was staying in bed with a headache? I found out later that my mum had been stood on the island in the road near Coalite where the picket line was. My mum and her friend had gone for a look before they went to work and a policeman told her to move saying she was 'causing an obstruction to traffic'. My mum refused. The short story of it is the policeman grabbed her, so my mum hit him and he called to six other policemen to put her in the van and take her to the police station. She was tricked into having her fingerprints taken and she had to go to court and was fined £75 for obstruction. The island has since been removed from the road.

My dad was also arrested and four of his ribs got broken and he wasn't well for a long time. He was fined for beating six policemen up, which is stupid and impossible as you'd know if you ever saw my dad. I really hated the police right then. I thought my dad was the best thing in the world and they had hurt him. I hated them! Which isn't a nice thing at all, a kid shouldn't hate the police, she should look up to them. A lot of people's attitudes changed through the strike. I live near the police station and that night people were gathered in crowds. It felt like the war when you see the Jews being pushed into a van and driven through people shouting and arguing. That night police vans were parked in the middle of the road-it took me a long time to get to sleep because their lights were shining into my bedroom. The buses couldn't turn round so they had to go up White City. I will always remember that night. The stupid thing is what I'll always remember about the strike is those shining brown shoes.'

I think I spotted Shaun Dooley first on TV as the vicar in *Eastenders* and thought – oh it's just the part for him; which is probably what every actor wants, but only for that moment in time. His view was, 'Soaps are great but shot so fast. You have less time to get things perfect circling work, travel home prep for the next day's shooting and then straight back at it. You have to be on top of your game the whole time'. More soaps, series and then with national impact in 2007 he is Trevor Reece-Jones the seat-belted surviving bodyguard of *The Last Days of a Princess*, and hits the button.

He masters the skill of taking the audience with him when he chooses to laugh at rather than with a character he plays; to hate them or absolutely adore them.

Characters one has loved, feared or loathed should be hard to forget, and Shaun Dooley's brutal, corrupt bullying Inspector in the 2009 TV production of David Peace's trilogy *Red Riding* was chillingly sinister enough to put him on hate lists forever. A shift to hard but good guy the same year for *Khandahar Break* but then back to *The Misfits* baby faced sociopath by 2012. 'It was a fantastic part and I was looking forward to being in it. We just spent every day filming and laughing, it was a very nice way to earn a living.'

It is I suspect that it was as Eddie in *Married, Single, Other* sandwiched between them that he left everyone, male or female, remembering his performance in the 2011 TV series and still asking why the series has not been followed up. From happy new husband and dad to grieving widower in one scene it was that lip-quivering reading of his late wife's last letter alone which was worth the BAFTA nomination it earned him. It put Mr Darcy's wet shirt in second place and every woman I knew was prepared to forgive him anything and everything.

His widely varied credit list is as long as your arm, and my Grandson who has just seen him in *Woman in Black* reliably informs me that he is 'really great'. The very private man that Shaun Dooley is would have none of that, as registering himself on LinkedIn as a full-time dad and actor/ writer might indicate. Genuinely self-effacing, when invited to do *An Evening With* at the Lamproom Theatre his text reply to me says it all,

'Are you sure? We could finish up just thee and me sat there having a natter on us own…'

And this lifelong Barnsley FC season ticket holding man who still does a 400 mile round trip to the Ponte End terrace for every home game he can make it to, would doubtless crack up to know that my spell-check has just auto corrected that to 'you and I'.

Born of generations of mining stock but when he didn't get the grades he needed to be a Vet, his dad's supportive as ever advice was that the pits were on their way out anyway, so he may as well be unemployed in trying to do something he loved doing. Now that early amateur dramatics experience he had with the family led him towards acting and enrolment at the Arden Drama School and a life of filming around the world with real life drama included. He lives by the rule that if a prospect scares him he should do it and likes pushing boundaries professionally and admits to having a dark sense of humour and a fear of being boring, mundane or predictable.

Star of stage, screen and television, Shaun Dooley. Photograph by kind permission of RANKIN.

Filming on the Pakistan/Afghanistan border four of the crew were shot in a terrorist attack and he nearly drowned making *Shackleton* in the Arctic on an ice breaker attached to a massive iceberg. Originally loving taking crazy options, now as a committed family man he no longer regards taking unnecessary physical risks as a responsible option.

His roots are deep as any pit, living in London is a rational decision, it's where availability of work is best located, but his views on bringing up his family there are tempered with built in adventure and freedom wherever possible. Valuing his own upbringing he recalls happy safe days building dens, playing football and wants his own family to share a full and healthy life without being mollycoddled. 'A good weekend for us would be spent doing things together as a family and travelling. We are all very adventurous.'

He will never be a 'luvvie' but a new shift is in place.

'I love the Cannes film festival; it's the fourth time I've been. I saw Sean Penn while I was there and he is one of my favourite actors. He was only about twenty yards away and I was a bit star struck. There were lots of famous people around.'

So says the man who doesn't know he has the same impact. Now writing is an alternative route to express his feelings, and with his first script picked up in a flash, he may be heading for a new career.

'It is a romantic comedy set in London. I can't say too much at this stage, it's my first feature film and I'm very excited. Cannes was amazing, I went as a writer and the film was picked up within three hours.'

I'm thinking that given his early start there's every chance that this could be where his next success lies so is it the future? Not necessarily it seems; as given the ultimate choice – saying he'd love to take over from Sir David Attenborough!

Chapter 4

A New Start in Grimethorpe

Part 1: All Change

In 1984 I had been seconded by Barnsley LEA from The Oaks School in Kendray to the Schools' Psychological Services. A far-sighted triage type initiative by Barnsley Education Department was already in effect in primary schools across the LEA comprising strategies for teachers to use in classroom situations to help them deal with physical, emotional, behavioural, social and learning problems. In line with the child-centred implications of the 1981 Act it was particularly appropriate timing as families, schools and whole communities struggled with the impact and additional complications of a year long miners' strike. My brief then had been to develop the material further and to introduce it for use in all of the authority's secondary schools, including those which before local government re-organisation had been West Riding Schools. Willowgarth High School in Grimethorpe was one, a 'Clegg School'; founded by and on the principles the renowned Educationist Sir Alec Clegg had always encouraged, and where inevitably learning through the Arts was at the core. Children were encouraged to draw, paint, act, love reading and to feel 'the excitement of writing' especially about what they experienced, observed, dreamed, feared and felt. In 1984 a Cambridge graduate, Max Bristowe, was Willowgarth's Head of English and already collating a timeless collection of children's writing aimed at both GCSE and CSE levels.

A microcosm of adolescence in a time of political upheaval, these accounts combined both the delightfully trivial and searingly revealing experiences these youngsters recalled.

If the views of these youngsters had been formally published at the time, who knows what hearts and minds they might have reached? As it was, when the next real life drama of 1992 hit the community, Max Bristowe would produce them as positive outcomes from a previously threatening situation to encourage others to record their feelings.

When I was first moved to work in 1990 Grimethorpe however, the situation was radically different. Relatively good times with guaranteed jobs, especially in the coal industry, had brought with them a slight air of complacency; and then major upheaval in terms of local authority educational policies ending the era of another Clegg initiative – Middle Schools. This was greatly mourned by those whose careers and teaching practice had been honed at that level.

Chris Davison was one:

'When schools in the West Riding of Yorkshire were taken over by Barnsley Council, the excellent middle schools in the Grimethorpe area knew that their time had come; it took Barnsley quite a long time to reorganise these schools, and their first schools into a conventional 5–11, 11–16 system; after we had been told at a meeting that there were no plans in existence to abolish the middle schools, we knew that the planning would start shortly afterwards! And we were right. So, some staff went to the junior schools and a few staff went into the new High School, where they would be teaching subjects instead of children. The senior schools probably didn't know what to expect, and I think they assumed that teaching children aged eleven or twelve would be pretty similar to teaching children aged 13 to 16. What they probably might not have realised was that the children from the Middle Schools had a strong sense of identity, a sense of pride and belonging because they had been in a small school where they were known and appreciated right up to the age of thirteen – they had indeed matured in a way they would not have done in a "conventional" junior school. A minor example of this phenomenon was that in the middle schools, pupils could already speak in French about events in the past; within a few years, this would be the prerogative of only the most able 5% of 16-year olds!

So, one September morning, these younger children arrived at their secondary schools to see only a few familiar faces among the staff, but on the whole, the children were thrown in straight away at the deep end of the secondary school system, and it would be very much different to what they had observed in their previous schools.

At Willowgarth High School, Grimethorpe, in 1990, there was some reorganisation at the top; maybe someone in higher authority had realised that it would not be sensible to expect the existing leadership to understand the needs, aptitudes and abilities of young people at a stage in their education which had never been their professional concern.

A deputy head teacher was appointed who had experience of children across the entire age range including what was becoming known as Years 7 and 8, and she understood that for the school to carry on in exactly the same manner as it had operated as a 13–18 establishment was probably not the right approach. She felt that the 'new' school (for such it was) needed to create for itself a distinctive identity, needed to inculcate in its pupils a strength of community at a difficult time in their own lives and in the life of the village; they should see that this was 'their' school.

Events which she organised were designed to further these aims – and to be fun! Principal among these were the compilation of a book in a day and the production of a drama about a nineteenth century mining disaster (in which the casualties were children of their own age and younger) and which had important consequences for the reform of child labour and mine safety. The 1993 production of the play *Children of the Dark* was first staged at the old Barnsley Civic Hall and later transferred to Sheffield Cathedral in the presence of the Archbishop of Canterbury, the Most Reverend George Carey. A book in a day attracted widespread publicity as did the Christmas Carols Service in Westminster Abbey and an International Women's Day exercise. These events served to show the children of Willowgarth that they were not alone, but part of a wider, indeed national, community. That Bishops and Cardinals, MPs and Mayors would be aware not only that this small village actually existed, but also that it contained children so talented in many ways could only enhance the self-esteem of the pupils, as well as making them very much aware of events outside their own villages.'

With over 600 new pupils and twenty-three new staff starting the school on the same day motivating new and existing students to aim even higher was not easy. Convinced that the rôle model approach begun at Darton High School in the 1970s remained valid, I asked a former pupil of Willowgarth for his help. Barry Cook readily agreed to present achievement awards in a modern version of the old style school Speech Day. As the first appointed Parent Governor at Darton High School over fifteen years earlier, he had observed and recognised the positive effect of role modelling work there and so became the first to support this new version.

A natural raconteur, he instantly engaged students, first talking about changes in educational opportunities since his own boyhood days; and that it was originally his former Craft teacher at Willowgarth, Stan Horton, who became his role model. Horton's personal integrity and professional commitment brought enjoyment of the practical subject, giving praise when it was deserved whilst teaching that success was really about hard work and respect.

At the end of his course however, like so many of his generation in coalfield areas, Barry Cook left school aged fifteen to become a trainee miner. Empowered by the excellent training and apprenticeships schemes then run by the National Coal Board, he put the hard work advice into practice becoming first a fitter then a foreman fitter before taking the leap in leaving the pit to become a salaried specialist representative with a national company providing equipment to the industry. Gradually building up knowledge of this end of the business emboldened him to take a further risk, that of setting up a business in factoring bolts and fastenings – largely for the mining industry.

That day in Grimethorpe however Cook Senior recalled days when he and his best pal first started work and as they walked to the pit, planned their big dream for the future. They would save up and buy a car together! It would have be a shared car they thought, as neither of them would ever be able to afford one of their own. This was after all, the 1950s, when such restricted aspiration was not uncommon.

By the time he re-visited his old school in Grimethorpe the business which he would eventually run with his son Dean bringing worldwide business to Barnsley, had already diversified and was coast to coast. Following his father's untimely death Dean Cook would take over and expand the business worldwide. He told his young audience that what skills and success as he had gradually acquired, resulted from working as hard as any miner had to. The message was flagged up loud and clear – that the only place where success before work is in a dictionary and it was in delivered in the straight-talking language they understood and accepted. There were already convincing local precedents in how successful balanced positive feedback could be. Sir Patrick Stewart is another perfect example of that brand of professional recognition; at every stage of his breathtaking career he has given credit to Cecil Dortmund, the teacher who first told him, 'You're good at this, Stewart, you should do more of it.' That one aside in a school inspired a youth with no theatrical background whatever, and sparked the belief that if someone he trusted thought that, then maybe he really could act.

Barry Cook's ongoing recognition of Stan Houghton's effect on his own development was a trigger for the next five years of positive rôle modelling which became a seminal part in motivating this particular mining community during some pretty tough changes. 1991 was also the Mayoral year of Cllr Ron Fisher who with his wife Christine, the Mayoress, took up the theme, frequently making supportive visits to the school. The Mayoress was particularly interested in promoting development through reading, with the aim of raising aspirations of girls who having less support at home had fewer opportunities to improve their reading skills and develop a love of literature. Often using her own relatively humble start in life as an example in what she astutely termed 'The Art of the Possible' she urged them to make and take every opportunity to make something of themselves. It was not the route so often sought now; dream about it and one day through luck or gimmick you might have fleeting celebrity.

One October day in 1992 started like any other in a school, routine timetabled diverse study, admin and activity. I had finished the attendance check, had meetings with two sets of parents, dealt with a report from staff that cars were obstructing bus duty by parking in the school drive and taken a call from the General Manager of the Yorkshire Traction Shafton Depot Alex Findley commending pupils for improved behaviour on the buses coming in to school. Then I had a call from Reception to say that a television journalist had just arrived and did I have time to see him. What Norman Rees wanted to know was how the fact that Grimethorpe pit was on the list of thirty-one Collieries that the Government had selected to be shut down was affecting the school.

That day ended with a national TV news bulletin featuring Chair of the Government's own Parliamentary Select Committee on Energy, Dr Michael Clark, Arthur Scargill, another Trade Union Leader and me. Equally strange was the fact that we all appeared to be holding fairly similar views – coal was sustainable as an industry and closure would lead to unemployment and economic disaster for whole communities. It was just another day, but like no other. Within twenty-four hours my diary was filled with names of bishops, actors, journalists and politicians, at the start of a rolling project which changed nothing – and everything!

Part 2:
Impact and Implications

It is a matter of record that I was born, educated, lived and worked in a mining town for all but three years of my life; and that my father and his four brothers, all miners, had worked at Grimethorpe Colliery at some point in their lives. I had happy childhood memories of Friday bus rides to Grimethorpe with him, sitting on the wall outside the main offices whilst he collected his pay or playing with other children whilst he had his hair cut in Albert White's barber's shop across the road. It was therefore predictable, if not inevitable, that I would have great empathy with and allegiance to that village. My main concern in October 1992 was the predictable impact on the educational potential of the children in the surrounding communities. As an English teacher, my personal concern was how to engage them in a creative response which would give voice to their feelings in a way which could at least prompt understanding and at best empathy.

The history was simple, Grimethorpe Colliery opened in 1893 and it was to be closed in 1992. Virtually every family in the area, if not personally employed, had family or friends there, or was part of the linked economy. The logic was less straightforward; there was a reported sixty-three million tons of coal remaining underground there, but strangely the pit was still on the closure list. This new crisis raised the bar to a perilous level and it was clear we would have to move swiftly, positively and proactively to minimise the inevitable damage. The positive potential was that it could become a perfect opportunity to follow on with Max Bristow's 1984 initiative, and bringing in parents and others in the community. We would go for support from wherever it was likely to be to open up opportunities for people to express their feelings in creative ways, but given my own bias would need to involve as wide a range of perspectives, beliefs and even politics as possible.

It was predictable that others would have a similar run of emotions. Local constituencies directly affected were likely to be first out of the traps, and they were. Jeff Ennis, Mick Clapham and Eric Illsley as the town's then longest serving Member of Parliament, but also Allen McKay and Terry Patchett, as well as local MEP Norman West. The strength and range of the immediate responses left us in no mind that it would be worthwhile

REFLECTIONS ON THE PROPOSED PIT CLOSURES (1992) FROM MY AUTOBIOGRAPHY — CLARK OF THE HOUSE (VOL II)

Sunday 18th October

Robin Cook (Labour - Livingston) telephoned me at home to discuss the wording of the motion he was proposing for the pit closure debate on the 21st. He wanted to make sure it was written in such a way that sympathetic Conservatives could support it.

I flew to Nice to chair the International Coal Conference; while in Nice I did interviews for BBC Wales and Thames TV about coal and the proposed pit closures.

Wednesday 21st October

A quickly arranged debate in the House on pit closures called by Robin Cook the Opposition spokesman on Trade and Industry in which I intended to speak. I spent the morning preparing my speech and at 2 p.m. met Peter McNestry the General Secretary of NACODS (National Association of Colliery Overseers, Deputies and Shotfirers) in the Central Lobby by appointment. I thought we would have a general chat but he had a specific request for me – 500 miners were gathered in the Methodist Central Hall, Labour M.P.s were supporting them but no Conservatives; would I go over? I agreed to do so on the condition that I did not have to wait to speak as I had to be in the Chamber by 3.30 p.m. in order to take part in the main debate. At St. Stephen's Entrance was a large crowd of miner's wives, the wives of the men I was going to address and one of them asked me if I was "the Tory M.P. that they had seen on the telly supporting the miners." I said I was and they gave me a huge cheer that was very emotional.

When I entered the back of the stage at the Methodist Central Hall a Labour M. P. was addressing the large audience of miners but Peter McNestry saw me and quietly introduced me to the leader of the TUC, Norman Willis who was chairing the meeting, and to the Bishop of Sheffield, who on learning that I was a Conservative said " Talk about Daniel in the lion's den !" Dennis Skinner (Labour) the aptly named "Beast of Bolsover" was waiting to speak, but Peter McNestry, true to his word, made sure that I was next. I went to the edge of the stage and peered into the gloom, seeing faces only in the first few rows but sensing the tension as the miners wondered how to greet a Tory. I had not had time to prepare a speech, indeed 40 minutes earlier I didn't even know that the gathering was taking place. I started something like this:

"I know that you are all wondering why at this time a Conservative M.P. is addressing this meeting. Well there are three reasons. I was until recently the Chairman of the Energy Select Committee and have studied your industry and know of its long term feasibility. Second, I believe your demands to retain your industry are justified, and finally I wish to support you because I was born and brought up in a coal mining area of Nottinghamshire", and they boo-ed and boo-ed. Peter McNestry leant forward and whispered to me that they were all NUM from Yorkshire – when they had been on strike seven years earlier the Nottinghamshire miners had broken away and formed their own Union, the UDM, and had continued working.

Amidst the boo-ing I had to think fast and as it subsided I said "Alright, alright, but I can't be held responsible for where my mother was when I was born, but I can be held responsible for where my wife was when our two children were born – she was in Yorkshire, so don't think of me as a Nottinghamshire man, think of me as a father of two Yorkshire kids", and they cheered heartily, listened to my speech and gave me warm applause at the end.

I spoke in the main debate in the House at 6.34 p.m., having earlier intervened on ~~Energy Select Council Hse~~ Michael Heseltine during his opening speech. I reminded the House – but really the Government - that we had recommended the continuance of the (E.S.C) as the House needed the ability to scrutinise energy matters as was apparent by the uproar which the pit closure

to ask him to tell us the difference between closing a pit and putting it into "review" which we all knew meant a delayed closure. He was embarrassed by my question.

announcement caused. I talked about the enthusiasm for coal at the Nice conference which I had chaired the day before, I reviewed reserves and advanced coal-burn technology and pointed out that the large redundancy payments proposed would be better spent on technology for the future – "I want more investment front-end in success and opportunity, not investment back-end on redundancy and failure"

Unfortunately the Government did nothing but propose that the Trade and Industry Select Committee look at the situation. I intervened on the closing speech of David Hunt (Conservative - Wirral West) the Industry Minister and as the Rev. Ian Paisley (Leader of the Democratic Unionists – Antrim North) said to me when he and I were voting in the Opposition lobby "As we say in Northern Ireland, if you hit the button the bell rings – you certainly hit the button". Robin Cook's motion, which we had been debating – an attempt to stop the pit closures – was defeated by 320 to 307.

Thursday 22nd October *Trade and Industry / Select Committee — Southend*

My stance, and that of others, was reported on the front page of *The Times* and the *Daily Telegraph* and later in the *Sunday Times*. Even *Time Magazine* carried my comments in a story about mining headed 'Shafted'. The *Evening Echo* devoted its editorial to the coal debate, kindly labelling me as a man of integrity, but slammed Major and the Government. The TISC met for the first time since the general election charged by the House to look into the coal industry. In fact the inquiry that followed was unnecessary as it was largely a repeat of the work done by the disbanded ESC. The Chairman of TISC, Richard Caborn (Labour - Sheffield Central) , asked me for assistance which I willingly gave, and relied heavily on my experience.

Monday 26th October

The day of my big lecture at the Royal Institution, by coincidence, so topical. I had been preparing the lecture and the 60 slides (I used on average one per minute) since the middle of the summer recess. My theme was clean coal technology, the essential contribution it could make to improving the efficiency of electricity generation and thus its beneficial effects on the environment and the survival of the coal mining industry.

The lecture was generously received. The Government's pit closure announcements had been very unpopular and my comments suggesting the retention **of** the coal industry by means of applying known and developed technology to coal-burn power stations received an unprecedented spontaneous mid-lecture round of applause. I finished almost exactly on time (one minute early) at 6.29 p.m. and was delighted by the welcome the presentation received. *from the coal industry professionals present and my fellow M.P's Kevin Barron, Geoffrey Dickens and Eric Illsley.*

as it soon became equally clear that there were actually few boundaries of class, creed, or political persuasion on seeing the support that flooded into the school. It became equally clear that further afield geographically there were pockets of total ignorance as to what the closures would actually mean to entire towns, villages and community life. What was not predictable was the level of support and even empathy from Westminster; the Commons, Government and Opposition as well as The Lords Spiritual and Temporal.

What was remarkable was that we had in agreement no less than the Chair of the Select Committee enquiring into the viability and sustainability of coal, Dr. Michael Clark. His diary from 18 October 1992 to Monday 26 October 1992, the week the closures were announced, indicates the findings of not only that committee, but also his bold personal stand in light of them.

And the word was really beginning to spread.

The original plan in my mind was to organise a permanent written record of memories and stories; the almost century-long history of the times Grimethorpe was a hardworking, thriving and essentially united mining community. We would gather memories, photos, views and recollections from as many as felt the need to express them and turn them into a book. I knew I needed advice so I rang friends for their reaction; acclaimed author Stan Barstow since the 150th anniversary of the Huskar Tragedy in 1988 had become a great friend and contributor to education in Barnsley. Having previously worked with Yorkshire Arts Circus on a community project based in The Oaks School, I also rang them. Stan's reaction was typical. 'Go for it – I'll bring a group of friends to help inspire and work with people.' The Arts Circus group offered their diverse experience to do the same and to help the English department in editing contributions to the book. The suggestion also came from the Arts Circus that to maximise publicity the book should be written in one day. The school's head and governors approved the plan and the word went out to the local community. Even though blogs, tweets and twitters were yet unheard of, within 24 hours the word had gone nationwide. The original plan had been for the school to invite members of the community and friends of the school to express and have recorded their own feelings and priorities as a massive scrapbook of memories. The new idea of gaining maximum publicity by doing the whole thing in a day brought in a pre-set chapter list from Yorkshire Arts Circus which was necessary to aid swift overnight editing which was done by them, as was the subsequent re-edit for publication. They worked to their usual system of not attributing names to individual contributions which meant many of the media-drawing celebrities were not identified and some were omitted from the completed text.

A note in my diary for the day indicates amongst the first to offer support, was Bruna Zamelli ringing with a message on behalf of Brian Glover who was 'very sorry that filming prevents him from being there in person, but he sends his very best wishes to you all for a great day and a successful outcome'.

It was only the day before the event in which we were to bring the community together to write the book, that I managed to get the number for Michael Parkinson's office. I explained the reason for my call to the lady who answered the phone and subsequently found I was speaking to Mary Parkinson. Her first response was actually a reflex as she already

1a.

23.10.92

Dear Chairman of Grimethorpe School,

Today I went with two miners from Grimethorpe to deliver a petition to the Prime Minister at No 10 Downing St. Fifteen thousand people had signed urging the Government to reconsider their decision to close down pits including Grimethorpe.

I went because my father worked for 50 years at the pit, and did his father. I grew up in Cudworth and started work on a local paper when I was 16.

I had a very happy childhood in a very close and caring community. I remember it well and because it meant so much to me I am concerned about its future.

I don't know if what we did today and what you and others are doing will make any difference. But we have to try and change things. Perhaps we can make Mr Major see sense. I hope so.

Good luck with your project.

Michael Parkinson.

knew beyond doubt that he would be delighted to help in any way he could. Proving the point she said he was not at home but then gave me his mobile number plus that of his tailor where, she said, he would be trying on his new suit.

He was, but that did not prevent him from taking my call and instantly offering to help in any way he could. Predictably, prior commitments meant that he was unable to attend the event on the following day, but he said he could and would send a copy of his latest book which included time his father spent working as a miner in Grimethorpe. He was as good as his word and the following morning the copy of the book duly arrived by courier in good time to be included.

There was also the following handwritten message to the children of Grimethorpe from the miner's son from 'Cudorth'.

As the word spread new and old supporters far and wide offered help, The Bishop of Wakefield, The Rt Rev Nigel McCulloch, Rita Britton of Pollyanna, Brian Blessed, Rodney Bickerstaffe, The President of Magdalen College Oxford, Barry Hines, with others, writers, actors, painters, pensioners and pupils. From Her Majesty's Inspectors of Schools to the Yorkshire Traction bus inspectors and drivers who daily brought the

THE BISHOP OF WAKEFIELD
The Right Reverend Nigel McCulloch

24 October 1992

Dear Children of Grimethorpe School,

On Wednesday I went with Grimethorpe Miners and families on the 'Flying Miner' train from Barnsley. When we got to London I marched in support of the miners, spoke at the big rally and, with the vicar and two Grimethorpe miners, had a special meeting at London House. Then, after lobbying parliament, I came back on the train with everyone to Barnsley.

I did this because I do not want Grimethorpe Colliery to close. I have read your letters to the Prime Minister saying it will be terrible if it does close. Congratulations on your excellent letters and all you've doing.

Keep up the fight.

God bless

✝ Nigel Wakefield

Bishop Nigel leads the Sharlston miners' march.
Photograph with kind permission of Jim Moran and *Yorkshire Post Newspapers.*

children into school, and hundreds of others giving what support they could; and it was tremendous.

So with such views from left, right and centre lining up together it did seem fairly clear that somewhere someone had got something very wrong.

It could be argued it was starting to look like an act of God. It was indisputably the speed with which he came on board, that the Bishop of Sheffield set another ball rolling starting when calling it 'People Power' he faxed me a copy of his diary dated 23 October 1992:

'What a week!

Tuesday: News of the closures begins to come through: strong resentment from the Bishop-"Sheer madness.... To close a pit which has good mineable coal is wicked... The policy of this closure must be stopped."

Wednesday: On every side the tides of public opinion were raging. People Power at work in Britain! Radio and TV give many opportunities. 'There must be a public uprising', says the Bishop. And there is.

Thursday: Start getting the Churches' petition going. Six hundred churches in South Yorkshire – of all sorts – ready to take part by Sunday.

Friday: Letters and letters: 'I never thought I'd support Arthur Scargill...!' 'I've been a Tory all my life, but...' 'I read your words in the Telegraph and from Dorset I just had to write...'

Saturday: Can we get the Electricity shareholders to do their stuff? Slowly that campaign starting to take off.

Sunday: Radio Oxford for Sunday program at 7 40am. Enthusiastic support for the miners from all students I met. Back to Sheffield in time for the Archbishop of York who backs the campaign strongly from the Cathedral pulpit. 72,000 people sign the petition.

Monday: The U-turn begins. Keep pushing!

Tuesday: Speech in the House of Lords. 'Coal is the fuel of the future. If it is not, if what we are being told is true – that these villages have to be destroyed; that these men have to go on the dole; and that there has to be a rather hopeless attempt at retraining and re-investing – then we need more convincing arguments that we have been given to date.' Government defeated by 125 to 100 votes.

Wednesday: Join with the Coalfields' Chaplain to meet Energy Minister. Rally in Central Hall Westminster...'

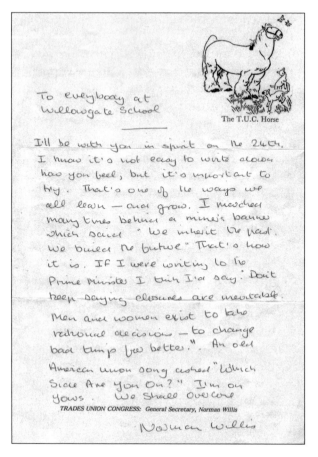

The T.U.C. Horse

To everybody at
Willowgate School

I'll be with you in spirit on the 24th.
I know it's not easy to write about
how you feel, but it's important to
try. That's one of the ways we
all learn — and grow. I marched
many times behind a miner's banner
which said "We inherit the past.
We build the future." That's how
it is. If I were writing to the
Prime Minister I think I'd say: Don't
keep saying closures are inevitable.
Men and women exist to take
rational decisions — to change
bad things for better." An old
American union song asked "Which
Side Are You On?" I'm on
yours. We Shall Overcome

TRADES UNION CONGRESS: *General Secretary, Norman Willis*

Norman Willis

'Restructuring Coal Mining' – Elizabeth Peacock's view:

'My big disagreement with the Major government arose in October 1992 on industrial policy and the re-structuring of the British Coal Industry. Suddenly without any notice Michael Heseltine announced the closure of thirty-one pits and the subsequent loss of around 30,000 coal mining jobs. I took serious exception to the way that this issue was handled. My problem was that there had been no meaningful investigation and discussion into the long term energy needs for Britain and what part coal was to play in competition with oil, gas and other sources. I accepted that many of the thirty-one pits were losing money and could not compete with imported coal and that a closure programme was necessary. My problem was the manner and speed of implementation so I had opposed government plans, making friends in the mining industry and enemies in the Conservative Party – I was back to rebelling. I indicated my unhappiness to the proposals to my whips stating that unless they were reviewed and the timescale of implementation was significantly modified I could not support the plan and would vote against.

My dilemma was that Ministerial responsibility was with Michael Heseltine who had made the initial announcement of the proposal. Michael had been a good supporter of my work in Batley and Spen having visited on several occasions and was instrumental in progressing Batley City Challenge funding. He had also been my choice of leader in the election when Mrs Thatcher resigned so I wrote to him explaining my position.

Elizabeth Peacock MP for Batley and Spen. Photograph by kind permission of Elizabeth Peacock.

This I did jointly with Winston Churchill pointing out our view that the government, together with Michael Heseltine and Tim Edgar, Minister for Coal, had got the process wrong and that the government should think again. The press were soon on the issue and all hell broke loose in the media, particularly when Roy Lynk, Leader of the Union of Democratic Mine Workers declared he would go on hunger strike down in the workings of the Silverhill Colliery, near Nottingham.

Winston and I decided that we should visit Silverhill to support Roy – which we did. Winston had already rung Brian Redhead on The Today programme before he set off for Silverhill and told him of our plans. Therefore when we arrived at Silverhill we were met not only by The Regional Manager of British Coal, but a mass of media people who had heard *The Today Programme.*

Understandably the Regional Manager refused our request to go underground but he did take us to the canteen where a great number of miners were meeting to consider the Government's proposals. When we joined them there we got a tremendous reception with TV cameras exposing the problem on a national and international level. Arrangements had been made for us to speak to Roy by the pit surface to coal face telephone system and we were able to assure him and everyone else present of our support.

We then did press interviews and photographs were taken for many newspapers and radio stations building on the story. The big question was 'why are you as Tory MP's supporting the miners' this was something many people just could not understand.

The answer was simple: 'our government has not adequately considered British energy policy especially the place of coal in the future mix. It must do so before we have a major restructure of British coal mining. We are not against restructuring but it must be done in a considered and controlled manner'.

On a personal level I did understand the position of the miners and the 1974 Heath government and the traumas of the industry after Arthur Scargill's defeat by the Thatcher Government in 1984. During this time I had worked with the then Coal Minister, David Hunt, and had arranged for working miners' wives to attend a meeting in the House of Commons to inform the Government of the very difficult circumstances that they were having to live with because their husbands wished to go to work. Their views, comments and photographs were taken directly to the Prime Minister by the Minister and I.

I did have great sympathy for those continuing to work during the strike.

Clearly Batley and Spen did not have any mines left but several local companies did supply equipment to the industry and needed to keep their manufacturing programmes running.

The TV and press coverage from Silverhill turned the whole issue into a national protest with me and a few other Conservative MPs as the leading protestors. Our attack on our own government came just as some poor economic figures were being published on production output and unemployment which turned the debate into an economic argument, thus widening the problem for Michael Heseltine and his team.

The Archbishop of York, Dr John Hapwood, called the proposed pit closures economic madness. Cardinal Basil Hume, the Archbishop of Westminster, wrote to Michael Heseltine saying he was 'distressed at the social and human costs of these drastic closures'.

The Labour Party demanded a statement and an emergency debate in the House or they would use their opposition day in the coming week to run such a debate.

Suddenly I seemed to become the unofficial spokesman for the

Tory protestors even though we had a Churchill on the team – maybe because I was the only woman or maybe because I gave them the story 'straight from the shoulder'. Wherever I went I was invaded by the media – on several occasions we had 2/3 TV or radio crews in our drive at home. I just could not escape. Almost everyday I had a telephone conversation with Michael Heseltine to see if we could find an answer and stem the rebellion which looked as though it could overturn the government.

An emergency debate was held with the Opposition pressing the need for a rethink but avoiding support for a possible miners' strike. I spoke in the debate saying "I am totally opposed to the wholesale closure of British coal mines, particularly in Yorkshire, until we have an agreed policy including coal together with oil, gas and so-called sustainable sources. Without this policy pit closures on this scale could be strategically dangerous for our economic future. It's fine to say 'we've got cheap imported coal at the moment but remember if we do close a mine it cannot be re-opened! In five years coal prices will have gone up and we will then be held to ransom by those countries on whom we have become dependent for our coal supplies."

A series of debates were held in the House on the issue. As the story unfolded and the government began to see some sense, I got some good support and an equal amount of abuse even from the Labour Party who I was likely to support. Having made a detailed speech setting out my position I was surprised to be attacked by Ron Davies, Labour Member for Caerphilly, who accused me of being undecided and that my claim to be an independent minded Yorkshire woman was no good if I was not strong willed and that he knew I would abstain. I was angry as I had no plan to abstain and tried to intervene in his speech but he would not give way. I appealed to the Speaker Betty Boothroyd but she could not help. To my further surprise, as I was being a nuisance to the Government, Michael Heseltine and David Hunt (then Secretary of State for Wales) took Ron Davies to task for his rude behavior. David Hunt saying "That was a disgraceful and discourteous speech, in the debate Mrs Peacock and Mr Churchill expressed concern about important issues yet the hon. Gentleman chose in an arrogant way not to give way and give them the opportunity to intervene".

Michael and David were gentlemen even though we disagreed!

Many other Tory MP's spoke on the lines of an economic problem. John Townend (Bridlington) called for further interest rate cuts, the former Trade and Industry Secretary Nicholas Ridley (now Lord Ridley) joined the argument from the Lords by warning of a 1930s style slump. John Carlisle (Luton) who was unhappy that Norman Lamont was still in place as Chancellor, despite the ERM debacle, used the coal argument to call for his resignation. All very confusing but following widespread public protests and our threatened revolt Michael Heseltine backed down temporarily and ordered a review. This kept the argument going for several weeks with me almost drowning in press interest. During this review and consultation period I visited Grimethorpe Colliery to meet local people and miners union representatives. Following this I went underground to the coalface at Maltby. In each case receiving a rousing reception for my support. I was receiving messages of support from around Britain and in particular from Yorkshire, including the then Bishop of Wakefield Nigel McCullough with his advisor the Rev Ian Gaskell.

I took both of them to a meeting with the head of British Coal to discuss the implementation of the plan. On the way to the meeting we very nearly needed a new Bishop of Wakefield because as we rushed across the road the Bishop was very nearly run down by the traffic -a fact he remembers to this day.

Michael Heseltine having accepted that the issue had been badly handled put the matter before the Commons Trade and Industry Select Committee. To take the furore away he provided lengthy consultations especially with the protesting Tories. I took part in this consultation process discussing the issue with Michael Heseltine. When he wanted to speak to me the phone would ring and a very important voice would say 'No.10 here' Mr Heseltine wants to speak to Elizabeth'. This worked well through my office but not so at home if my husband answered the phone as he had got tired of the performance. When the voice said 'No.10 here' he would reply 'No 10 where?' and then await the reaction at the other end which was often frosty.

One day my office reported that a Mr Scargill had been on the phone saying he would like to meet me and would I go to his headquarters in Yorkshire for a meeting. We replied happy to meet but it would have to be at my office in 1 Parliament Street. This meant with our House security we would not have a media scrum ensuring that there would be no publicity. So the very next day Arthur Scargill arrived in my office for a discussion on mine closures and the future. He opened the discussion by saying he was not entirely happy discussing the topic with a Conservative member of parliament but believed he had no viable option if the closures were to be stopped or slowed down. Arthur was a perfect gentleman, we had a sensible discussion over a cup of coffee. I emphasised that I was not against re-structuring the industry which would require some closures but I was totally opposed to the way the government was proceeding. Obviously he could not agree to restructuring but thanked me for my efforts on behalf of his members.

At long last after weeks of consultation the government decided to proceed as planned starting with another debate in the House and a vote. The speculation on the days leading up to the debate and vote was that it would be a close run thing for the government. However, I knew that some of the early Tory protestors now considered that the government had reviewed energy policy and the proposals in sufficient depth for them to abstain or even vote with the government. I was not convinced that our energy policy had been studied in sufficient depth and the demand for coal quantified. I therefore announced my continued intention of voting against the government.

To my horror, early on the day of the Debate and vote my House of Commons Secretary, Lorna, rang to say that Alistair Campbell in his column in the *Daily Mirror* that morning was saying that I had changed sides and would vote with the government. He then suggested all miners and their supporters should ring my office telephone to express their disgust. He then provided my House of Commons internal office telephone number and so many angry and in some cases obscene calls came in. So much so that the Sgt-at-Arms closed down the switchboard completely for a short period to relieve the pressure.

As my husband, Brian, was in London I discussed with him what action should be taken to ensure the truth was told long before the vote was taken. I felt, at that time, unable to deal with Alistair Campbell and needed to concentrate on my speech for this important debate. In response Brian organized a press release re-confirming my intention to vote against the government, and adding that we intended to instruct solicitors to sue the *Daily Mirror* and Campbell. This went to all Radio and TV stations within the hour.

He then rang the *Daily Mirror* and Campbell to confirm our action.

After some difficulty he did get through to Alistair Campbell and after an exchange of some basic Yorkshire language Campbell agreed he had got the story completely wrong and that the *Mirror* would change the story in their later edition and taking out my telephone number and they would apologise in print later. To be fair they did apologise somewhat belatedly but well after the event.

Throughout the whole of this drawn out affair I had remained PPS to Nicholas Scott, Minister for the Disabled and continued working on his behalf. The convention was that when a member of the government team votes or threatens to vote against government they should resign their position.

As a PPS is a very small cog in the government wheel I told Nick Scott, subject to his agreement that I did not intend to resign before the vote as I had not yet committed the crime! He was very understanding and as I knew he would not sack me I carried on working with him.

During the debate the issues were aired again and I repeated my position. However, the protestors reduced in number so the government won the vote with a majority of thirteen, six Tory rebels voting with the Opposition, with five other Conservatives abstaining. My colleagues who held their resolve to the bitter end and voted against the government were Richard Alexander (Newark) Dr Michael Clark (Rochford) Richard Shephard (Aldridge Brownhills) Nicholas Winterton (Macclesfield) and Ann Winterton (Congleton).

The five abstaining were David Nicholson (Taunton) Toby Jessel (Twickenham) Peter Fry (Wellingborough) Sir Richard Body (Holland with Boston) and Sir Patrick McNair – Wilson (New Forest). These colleagues were not convinced that the government had gone far enough with their concessions but would not vote against.

Eight Ulster Unionists [who would normally vote with the government] also abstained and were the subject of much ridicule from Labour MP's.

I had voted with the Labour Party before but some of my fellow rebels found it a 'different experience'. My greatest disappointment during the debate and subsequent vote was when Winston Churchill announced that the government had now done enough to satisfy his concerns and that he would vote with the government.

My reaction was 'Turn Coat'! as I was disappointed for the miners. However I had been warned that Winston might change his mind as he had used this sort of tactic before. Eventually I got over my disappointment and as he was my office neighbor we remained friends until his untimely death.

As the result of the vote was announced I headed across the lobby to meet the press, as I had agreed earlier. On the way out of the Chamber I was met by the Conservative Duty Whip Nicholas Baker (Dorset) who was obviously waiting for me saying simply "Elizabeth you're sacked forthwith as a PPS" my reply was "I was about to resign!" and on I went to meet the press. The very first press question was "Elizabeth when are you going to resign as a PPS? My reply was "I don't need to, I have just been sacked!

The BBC who had been covering the vote on TV flashed up my photograph at the end of the 10' 0 clock news with a subtitle "Rebel Yorkshire Tory MP sacked for supporting miners". This caused comment for days in the media.

Some people in the Conservative Party were not happy with the way I had supported the miners and some who have never forgiven me for the part I played. In my view governments have to learn that they must prepare their ground and take their supporters and the people with them as they formulate policy and action. The government did not do this when announcing pit closures so I opposed and would do so again in similar circumstances. I certainly understood the Party view the next day when I met Virginia Bottomley in the Members Lobby when she told me in a very loud voice what a disgrace to the Conservative Party I was. Unfortunately for her she did so in the hearing of the badge messengers and some Labour MPs who reacted by saying she had gone too far. Similarly I believe it was my efforts to force the Government to review energy policy and my support the miners that upset the late Alan Clark and encouraged him to make two disparaging remarks about me in his 'Diaries', which then reached the newspapers. I reacted by saying I did not think much of him either, that he was a terrible snob and philanderer who lived on his families' financial success. Maybe he was an old fashioned Tory but never a modern Conservative!

Some years later I did get the opportunity to get a little revenge for his Diary comments when Alan Clark who had given up his Plymouth seat suddenly wished to return to the House as Member for Kensington and Chelsea replacing my old boss Sir Nick Scott who had died. When Alan was unexpectedly selected as the Conservative candidate I was asked by a Yorkshire newspaper to comment which I did in the following manner under the headline "How could Party pick this reprobate". I said I thought it unbelievable that anyone would choose this self confessed philanderer, reprobate and adulterer. I said he was an unpleasant and arrogant man who was extremely rude about the North and people in trade.

Which was surprising as he was not a true aristocrat – his family made their money in the cotton trade. His comments about Michael Heseltine having to 'buy his own furniture' was the last word in arrogance.

My View

Looking at the issues now some twenty years on with a clearer eye and less emotion I can say:

Yes the British coal mining industry had to be rationalised and re-structured, even Arthur Scargill knew that, but could not say so. Many of the pits were inefficient and losing huge amounts of tax payers money. The cost of taking coal from these inefficient British deep mines was considerably greater than international open cast coal and therefore restructuring had to happen. The question was when and how.

The Government's timing in Autumn 1992 was probably correct. Michael Heseltine and Tim Eggar got the 'how' bit wrong. They should have had the energy review first then announced the rationalization programme. Michael is a big picture businessman who clearly said to Tim Eggar (Coal Minister) "get the industry re-structured and privatised now". Eggar did not put in the detailed review work required and just pushed on regardless.

His personal style upset the coal industry, the politicians and others who reacted with vigour.

The proposal could and should have been handled better but the government got their way in the end, 10 mines were closed and the remains of the industry privatised.'

In full agreement with Elizabeth Peacock was no less a person than Eton and Oxford educated Winston Churchill, Member of Parliament for

Levyhulme, then Stretford. Perhaps he was aware of a World War Two promise his grandfather had made to British miners on 22 April 1943:

'One will say, "I was a fighter pilot"; another will say, "I was in the Submarine Service"; another "I marched with the Eighth Army"; a fourth will say, "None of you could have lived without the convoys and the Merchant Seamen" and you in your turn will say with equal pride and with equal right, "We cut the coal".'

 RT. HON. JOHN SMITH QC MP

HOUSE OF COMMONS LONDON SW1A 0AA

Press Notice

MESSAGE TO GRIMETHORPE SCHOOL FROM THE RT HON JOHN SMITH QC MP, LEADER OF THE LABOUR PARTY

The disgrace of this government's action against Britain's coalfields has outraged the nation, not only those involved in the industry but people from all walks of life who understand the needless suffering these closures will bring, and who know our country cannot afford redundancies on this scale or the loss of this strategically vital energy resource.

I am sure today's worthy event at Grimethorpe School will raise the public profile of the miners cause. It saddens me to see a small community such as yours, suffer because of such a callous government decision. The people of Grimethorpe and threatened coal communities throughout the country deserve better.

You can be sure that as leader of the Labour Party I will do my utmost to fight for the survival of our coal industry. In campaigning to halt the pit closures, with the backing of people throughout the nation, we will urge John Major's government to think again about this disastrous decision.

I hope the day goes well and helps to highlight the just cause we are all fighting for.

ends

An ex miner himself at the age of fourteen, Lord Mason of Barnsley told me of a House of Lords debate following Lord Ezra's call for an independent enquiry into the Government's proposal for pit closures. Lord Jenkins, who once referred to himself as 'working class squirearchy', had challenged Baroness Denton's announcement that the Government 'saw no possible logic in a demand for more than 45 million tonnes of coal'.

19 October 1992 *Hansard* records 'That is tangled up with a curious competitive structure in relation to the electricity industry, and to some extent the gas industry, which arises out of the method of privatisation that the Government chose to pursue. Unless there is an enquiry into the whole matter to try to disentangle the position there will merely be a stay of execution without a hope of survival.'

Baroness Denton of Wakefield's reply to that was that coal was being mined 'for which there is no market'.

Lord Mason of Barnsley's response was twofold – the timing and manner in which the announcement had been made, and the apparent lack of logic in the statement. He denounced it as totally irresponsible and now seen as a panic-stricken measure:

'It was delivered in a cowardly fashion while Parliament was in Recess. It was monstrous as it is, with such serious national implications and with repercussions reverberating all around the country that was not agreed by the Cabinet. That statement outraged the nation. One can now readily see what a callous, insensitive uncaring statement it was. Most Conservatives have been ashamed. The miners and their families are shocked and incensed. The whole nation feels aggrieved.'

Refusing to yield the floor he continued:

'My Lords, even now, we have not yet had a reasoned presentation from the Government, who are still determined that the coal industry is virtually to die. This is only a temporary pause is it not? Yet we import 20 million tonnes of coal annually. Why? It is foreign coal. We are importing unemployment.'

He then proceeded to question what he regarded as serious miscalculations:

- 20,000 tonnes of foreign coal = 20,000 miners' jobs
- Britain importing nuclear power from France = output of five coalmines = 5,000 jobs
- Closure of mines which produce the cheapest coal in Europe whilst competing with heavily subsidised nuclear power and German coal.
- Job losses
- Energy costs
- Energy deficits in the balance of payments
- Future security of supply
- Cost in terms of unemployment benefit and lost tax revenue

In an attempt to swing the subject back, Baroness Denton, who was also a Director of British Nuclear Fuels, expressed surprise that Lord Mason had raised the subject of imports as 90% of coal used in power stations was from UK mines. The comeback to that was from the former educationist Lord Dormand of Easington. The impeccably courteous, unflappable and universally popular Durham, Loughborough and Harvard educated member simply asking, 'Why not 100%?'

That was sufficient to bring to his feet one of my personal favourite parliamentary characters – the witty and charming hereditary peer, The Earl of Onslow:

'May I congratulate the Government on doing something which I believed to be impossible – to ally the middle classes of Surrey and the rest of the South of England with Arthur Scargill and make them his Fan Club?

But is it not true – that the Government's judgement on this matter has been seen to be badly lacking? It is essential that there should be a proper inquiry into whether the market for fuel for electricity generation [sic] has been rigged, which is what appears to be the case when one reads the newspapers. To ask us to trust the Government's judgement at the moment is, I am afraid to say and I do not like saying this as a Conservative, not very pleasant.'

Baroness Denton, from her start at Rothwell Grammar School and the London School of Economics, had been a uniquely brave and bold inspiration to women aspiring to succeed in worlds which were then still virtually male territory. Not only in marketing, commerce and local government, nor as the first woman to serve on The Institute of

Management, she was also the first woman appointed as a Minister at Stormont. As a universally respected rally driver she completed the London to Sydney Rally in 1967 – driving the only sports car in the event. She helped found and chaired Forum UK from 1989 to 1992 and was part of its involvement with the International Forum for Women through which I first met and applauded her for such contributions. In regular visits to the North she had become an inspiration to another of its icons, Rita Britton.

But in early 1993 when Baroness Denton last visited Pollyanna in Barnsley after lunch and happy chat, as she was leaving Rita Britton presented her with a copy of a book in a day.

'Oh that's bit under the belt!' exclaimed Baroness Denton.

And straight back came the riposte from the woman who at 6am had been amongst the first visitors through the school gates to have her 'two pennorth' on the day a book in a day was written.

'Yes, that's exactly what we thought about the pit closures...'

Rita Britton, great supporter of Willowgarth High School's battle against the pit closures.
Photograph by kind permission of John Britton.

Part 3:
Letters to the Prime Minister

The threat of impending closure obviously did not escape the children. From their feelings, increasingly expressed in school, it was easy to imagine the conversations that were taking place in homes across the catchment area. Despite there being no set policy to involve the children it was extremely difficult to avoid hearing their views and it was impossible to ignore their daily concerns. After spontaneous verbal accounts some youngsters opted to write letters of complaint to the office they held responsible – though in some cases it is more than clear that in their views one individual was to blame. Some wrote about their own family's fear, others supported friends or neighbours, some saw a wider perspective and attempted diplomacy, tried awareness raising by appeals to a better nature and even the sympathy vote . Some naively suggested an unawareness or heedless lack of thought in political pre-planning, or were youthfully ironic whilst others went for blatant sarcasm. But with one voice all questioned what rationale could threaten such radical change in their own lives – or that of their community.

Dear Mr. Major,
I am ashamed of a fellow Chelsea F.C. supporter, that supporter is you. I thought myself that you would be the right person for the Prime Minister job, but I have changed my mind. Everybody is disappointed at your decision about Grimethorpe, especially the miners and their families. My friend's brother john works at the Coalite, John is disgusted at your actions and so are other people who are employed by Coalite. I ask you, would you shut the pits if your family worked or lived in Grimethorpe? I hope when you see the thousands of letters against the closures you see sense; the sense is to think of the people and keep the pits open.
Boy aged 12.

Dear Prime Minister,
I think you have made a bad decision closing down Grimethorpe pit. You are putting lots of people out of their jobs. All the truck drivers will have no jobs. All the people who have lost their jobs will have to look for new ones. And jobs are hard to come by. There will be a lot of people out of work and on the dole. It does not bother my dad because he works for himself. But it bothers me a lot. I will not get a job because all the jobs will have gone to the people who have been looking for jobs for years, and when I get old enough to vote I will not, I will say this only once, I will not vote for YOU! And I will be grateful for you to leave Grimethorpe pit open.
Boy aged 12.

Dear Mr. Major,
I am writing to you to, er how can I say this? I am writing to you to tell you my views on your closing down of Grimethorpe pit Mr. Major, my step father works there as a fireman. I really need him as my own father died there. I don't want to go into why but we need the money. We are a poor family and I hope you will notice that Grimethorpe is a poor village. If the pit closes it will be a great loss as we need clothes, food, and a home. I know you will not be taking much notice, you might not be even reading my letter but I am pleading with you, please don't close our pit. If you do people will leave our village, as there will be no work in Grimethorpe. It will eventually be a ghost town. Why don't you close a different pit in a richer town where people who lose their jobs won't starve? Please don't close Grimethorpe pit.
Girl aged 11.

Dear Mr. Major,
I am writing his letter in concern for the closure of the Grimethorpe colliery. I live in Shafton, which is one of the surrounding villages of Grimethorpe, and am very worried and upset and annoyed at the decision to close the pit. My family is not a mining family but a lot of my friends have mining families. If the closure goes ahead Grimethorpe will slowly die, shops will have to shut down as no one will have any money to spend in them. Also people won't be able to sell up and move away because nobody will buy their houses. Pubs,

shops and small businesses will close down. The crime rate will rise in surrounding villages because people will feel they need to steal to get money. Please reconsider the closure.
Girl aged 12.

Dear Mr. Major,
I think you made a very bad decision closing down the pits because that means there will be a lot looking for jobs and they will be looking for a very long time. When I get older I will not get a job because you have shut all the pits and offices and when I get older I will never vote for you. I wish you would open all the pits again because when I was little I always wanted to get a job at the pit but now you have shut the pits I can't can I?
Boy aged 12.

Dear Mr. Major,
Why shut down 31 pits? My dad has worked at Grimethorpe Colliery as an assistant surveyor, a couple of months ago he got his redundancy so left. He may have got his money but yet 30,000 others didn't. One is my uncle who has a two-year-old child. His wife has a decent job at Doncaster Hospital but still they need money to help pay for, sometimes babysitting, Christmas, people's birthdays and if things break, to replace them. They also have a dog, cat and two budgies to look after, also bills to pay. They still have quite a bit to pay on the house and car they will only just have enough money coming in, especially with a two-year-old to pay for everything. Also a friend of mine's dad works at the pit, he has two children aged ten and twelve to look after and his wife only has a poorly paid job to look after them with. Sometimes I wonder if this government is any good. After all a lot more jobs will go what with the railways, metal and machine makers, and what for because there is still quite a lot of coal left. Also it will probably cost as much if not more to close them down as to keep them open. Why waste money and coal and add to Britain's ever growing number of unemployed.
Boy aged 12.

Dear Mr. Major,
I am writing to let you know how the closure of the Grimethorpe colliery is going to affect me and my family. I live across the road

from Grimethorpe colliery. My father is a retired miner and we get coal from the pit, we fear that if the colliery closes we might lose our coal. I am also a member of the Grimethorpe Colliery 'B' Band and the band may have to break up. We have the best band in the world in Grimethorpe. The shops up the road from where I live will probably close and we will have to travel to Barnsley just for a loaf of bread. I've written to bring your attention to this issue and how it will affect the whole village and not just the miners.
Girl aged 12.

Dear Prime Minister,
I am very sorry to notify you like this but I think that you are making a very big mistake in your decision. I am very worried about you closing the pits because the people who have children will be out of work and they do like to get up in the morning for work you know. My dad works at the pit and he gets up in the morning at 5am for work and I will be sad if the pit closes. I do not want to go to school shop for my school clothes and I do not want to go on school tokens. So please let them work for their families. I have been watching the news and I think that it is wrong to let the pit go. My dad works every day and night to make us a family. Please let my dad go on working.
Girl aged 12.

Dear Mr. Major,
Most people in our school will be affected by the pit closures, Emma my friend will be affected because her dad works in the pit. People will not be able to pay their poll tax or other bills. People have worked hard over the years so please DO NOT CLOSE THE PITS. It will affect my dad because it will make it harder to get a job and he has been trying to get a job for two years now and he has not got one yet.
Girl aged 11.

Dear Mr. Major,
I am writing to you as a concerned pupil of Willowgarth High School. The pit is the main source of jobs in our area so many families will be out of jobs and us the children when we grow up will have less chance of getting a job. Many of the miners will not be able to find another job and the miners who do will not earn that

much, or they will be on the dole. In the time the colliery will be dangerous please don't close the pit.
Boy aged 13.

Dear Mr. Major,
I am writing against the pit closures in my area, many people will lose their jobs and their lives will be ruined. You are well aware of the fact that many power stations are changing to gas and new clean power but we only have a few years supply and this is much dearer than coal, coal in many parts of England and Wales is plentiful. If the pits were to close the area would be a ghost town with people looking in other areas for jobs. What jobs will there be for children such as me when I grow up? The redundancies and other money to be paid out for the closures of the pits will be in the millions. Just think for one moment – is it worth it?
Boy aged 13.

Dear Mr. Major,
I am truly concerned about the closing of Grimethorpe Colliery and Houghton Main. Many of their employees are disgusted by your drastic action to close the pits so near to Christmas. I am surprised how badly you are treating people. Many of the employees will wake up soon to find there is nothing to get up for. They also have families how could need urgent attention such as little babies and there will be no provision for them. I attend Willowgarth High School and each of the communities around Grimethorpe is going to stop at nothing to keep the pit open. It's not only going to be the pits out of work, but also the manufacturers that supply the pits with parts for machinery or the machinery itself. The pit In Grimethorpe is the only thing keeping the village going. Many people are to be redundant and with so many jobs going, just think of the children who are taking exams soon to leave school and what are they going to face? UNEMPLOYMENT. Please reconsider your decision, as you don't know how many people you are hurting.
Girl aged 13.

Dear Mr. Major,
I am a pupil of Willowgarth High School. We have been discussing the matter of the closure of the pit at Grimethorpe. I feel that all of

the pits should be kept open because it seems like lots of money has been wasted as you have just spent millions of pounds on refurbishing all the pits and it is cheaper to produce coal in England than it importing it from abroad. Also lots of miners have been made redundant and some are too old to get other jobs and it is the children that will suffer. The crime rate will increase because people who have been made redundant will begin to steal as there wont be much money. You will not only be putting the miners out of a job but lot of other people too, for example coach painters because families wont be able to afford to on holiday on the bus companies wont have enough money to have their coaches painted, also coal merchants because there wont be coal to deal in.
Girl aged 13

Dear Mr. Major,
I am concerned about the welfare of the employers of Grimethorpe pit. I myself have no relatives who work at the pit, but most of my friends have fathers and uncles who work very hard at the pit. They have worked for years to provide money for their families. Most of the men that work there don't know how to do any other job but work at the pit, they have no experience with any other job. Senior citizens (who have coal fires) will not be able to afford a gas fire because they may not be able to use the technology gas fires require because they are used to coal. Why do you want to put hundreds of men out of work here? Think about your next election, people wont want to vote for a person who put them out of a job! Please, please reconsider thinking about closing Grimethorpe Pit.
Girl aged 13.

Dear Mr. Major,
Please could you keep Grimethorpe pit open. Many of the employees are going to be made redundant because of the closure. Many families will be deeply distressed over the closure and lots of other people will become unemployed if Grimethorpe has to close because local people would not be able to afford the money to purchase goods. Grimethorpe will become a ghost town because nobody will not need to go thorough it anymore. Grimethorpe put is also the cheapest in the country for its coal. It is going to cost more to close the pit than it would to keep on running it. Please could you reconsider your decision?
Girl aged 13.

Dear Mr. Major,
I am not very pleased about what is happening to Grimethorpe pit.
My mum and Dad have not been getting any sleep because of the
closure of Grimethorpe pit. My dad has been working and *towing
his rops* out at Grimethorpe pit since he left school at fifteen years
old. When the ten pits do close they might not get their redundancy
till Christmas. When Christmas comes we will not have any money
to buy presents. Please do not close the Grimethorpe pit.
Girl aged 11 uses local dialect colloquialism for working as hard as
is humanly possible.

Dear Mr. Major,
I am a pupil of Willowgarth High School and I am worried about
my dad and his job. The reason why I am worried is because my dad
works at the Carlton Main brick works. I am worried that this pit
closing business is going to interfere with my dad's jobs. I don't
know if it will or not but I am very worried it might and I am
concerned about other people as well. Everyone in Grimethorpe or
anyone who works at the pit they are all going to be out of jobs.
Most of the shops and super markets are going to close down
because they cannot afford to keep them open and cannot afford to
pay other people who work for them, why can't you just think?
What would you do if you were not the prime minister and you
worked at the pit? You and all your friends lost their jobs over a
stupid thing like this and there was no were else to go, you would
have no money and no jobs and it would be awful. Please just have
a really good think about people and their jobs and their futures and
not just money please give it a second thought.
Girl aged 12.

Dear Mr. Major,
We are pupils are Willowgarth High School. We are asking you to
reconsider your decision of closing Grimethorpe Colliery pit. It does
not only affect the miners and office staff lorry drivers etc, but it
affects the whole community. Lots of people including relatives of
us both have worked there for many years and it is all they know. A
lot of miners are too old to get another job. The redundancy money
may cover the cost of living for a few years but what happens when
the money runs out, how will they feed and clothe their families

then? A dole cheque every fortnight is not the same as a regular income. We are asking you not just to save the pit but to save the community of Grimethorpe and its surroundings.
Girl aged 14 and girl aged 14.

Dear Mr. Major,
Thank you for closing the pits. Thank you for destroying over a hundred years of tradition. Thank you for making over thirty thousand people unemployed. Thank you for destroying the community. Thank you for spoiling thousands of kids' Christmas. Thank you for taking my dad's only source of income, well done you deserve a pat on the back. I hope you sleep well tonight because I know 30 thousand people who won't.
Boy aged 14.

Dear Mr. Major,
I go to Willowgarth high School in Grimethorpe near Barnsley. After hearing that you are closing the pits and other ones around the region I think you should listen to the public. It is disgusting what you are doing to the pits and hundreds more people agree with me, we think you should reconsider what you are doing. What are people supposed to do to earn a living? You don't live around these people you can't see what you are doing to them by your heartless decision. Grimethorpe colliery was a slice of history to Grimethorpe people and it will be a disaster if you destroy it. It's okay for people like you, you can have a secure job but what about others. All the blame is put upon you and Michael Heseltine. Don't you think you should reconsider? Because we do!
Girl aged 14.

Dear Mr. Major,
I am writing to you about the closure of the pits, my father has worked at Grimethorpe colliery for twenty-fve years, he is a hardworking man like most of the miners, after going underground for years I don't think miners should have to resort to a life on the dole as most of them will after the pit closures. Most of the men have no skills other than working down the pit so it will be hard for them to get an alternative job. On the day when they announced all the pit closures my father was deeply upset and warned us about

our family's future if he will be able to get another job. Also my uncles and cousins who have lost their jobs are worried as well, so the closure of the pits will affect most of my family very badly and also my friends' families. What will happen to the boys who are going to school now? What jobs will they have to go to when they get older? In this area many followed their fathers and grandfathers into the pits. I feel very strongly about the situation but I feel nothing that I say will make you change your mind, but I just hope it helps you to understand the public's feelings.
Girl aged 15.

Dear Mr. Major,
I would like to ask you first of all to reconsider the action to close the pits especially Grimethorpe. My brother works at the Coalite next to the pit in Grimethorpe and if Grimethorpe closes the Coalite would have to get coal from elsewhere. Mr. Major, was any of your fore fathers a miner or anything to do with the mining society? If so, how would they feel if they had the choice, what do you think they would say? The choice is yours and all you have to do is think of the people in Grimethorpe and don't close our pits, if you do the people in the community may say 'John Major helped us to keep our pit open.' I will hope that my letter and thousands more will help to change your decision.
Boy aged 13

Dear Mr. Major,
I am very upset about the mines closing down. It has upset my dad and other relatives. Thousands of jobs will be going down the drain. They will all be out of work, so please don't close the pits down for my sake as well as thousands of others children too. It isn't very fair we won't get as many Christmas presents because we won't have enough money. It doesn't matter to you because you won't be out of a job you don't know how it feels because tories have got lots of money. Some miners have broken down in tears,, and one man even went down to the pit and said he wasn't coming back up because he knows he will be out of a job. It is very hard to find another job please, please reconsider closing down the pits.
Girl aged 11.

Dear Mr. Major,

Why are you closing these pits down? There will be thousands and thousands of people out of work. They will have the worst Christmas they would have had in their lives especially for their families. There will be so many people redundant, all or and, spare jobs will be taken and there will be hardly any jobs left for the new generation. It will be like ghost town, with no one in the houses, because they will be in the streets. It will destroy some people.

Boy aged 12.

Dear Mr. Major,

I am writing to you because I am deeply concerned about your decision to close Grimethorpe pit. A lot of pupils who attend Willowgarth High School have parents who are miners. If the pit closes the parents will be out of work and therefore will have no money, apart from dole money to buy their uniforms, pens, pencils etc. A disused pit can mean injuries by bits of metal and other debris left lying around. If the pit does close at least three times as much dole will have to be paid out to ex miners. If Grimethorpe pit does close most of the businesses in the village will go bankrupt through lack of trade from miners, yet more dole to pay out.

Boy aged 13.

Dear Mr. Major,

I am writing on behalf of many concerned and anxious people who ask the question – why? Why are you trying to destroy one of Yorkshire's greatest working industries? Why are you jeopardising the future of thousands of families both directly and in-directly? Why are you putting so many miners on the line and not the chairperson? Some of the people lives whose you are wrecking will have mortgages etc. surely so many families wont be able to survive on the dole? Why not think again?

Girl aged 15.

Dear Mr. Major,

I am writing this letter to you to tell you my views on the pit closures. My father is a fitter down the pit and so I know how hard miners work. There are no people that I know of that are more dedicated to their work than miners are. The pit closures will affect

The Prime Minister.
10 Downing Street,
London.

Dear Mr Major,
          I am writing to you
about the closure of Grimethorpe pit.
The miners are very depressed about
the decision you have made. You
will make a lot of redundancies
and families will suffer from that
              All the people are
deeply concerned about your
decision. How would you feel
if you were a miner and someone closed your pit? Please just reconsider your decision to close
the colliery.
              Times are bad enough
anyway for parents in the recession
you have made, so come on, and
don't close the pit, it would
save a lot of distress to people.
                    Yours sincerely
                      D. Smith (13 years)

P.S Sorry about the mistake, we
       all make them!

young people as well as old, and men will be unemployed which could bring lots of grief upon families with young children who do not understand the difficulties these jobs losses will bring. Difficulties such as money shortages due to no wages put pressure on marriages even leading to possible divorces, meaning children in these circumstances will suffer emotional disturbances. Areas of high unemployment suffer from a higher crime rate which will cost tax payers more money than the right amount of policing for that area, and the government already says they can't afford to put more police in these areas now so what is going to happen in years to come when the crime rate increases and we have no extra police cover? The government will have millions of pounds to pay in dole money and benefits to men who would rather have pride in working for a living. Men could lose their homes when they can no longer pay their mortgages leaving people homeless, putting more pressure on taxpayers to find hotels, hostels and council houses for these homeless families. People on the dole don't pay tax to the government so it will lose thousands of pounds a week in lost taxes. In areas of high unemployment businesses will fold as people have less money to spend, this will make more people redundant and unemployment will escalate. Apart from the miners' jobs lost other people's jobs will go too, people who work in pit laundries, caterers, canteen staff, office staff, transport staff and office cleaners. Companies supplying machinery and steel, ropes, chains, tools and wood all these have not been taken into consideration. You are not just closing mines you are closing communities.

Girl aged 15

But he wasn't swinging their way, despite the plethora of common sense and economic mayhem.

To the best of my knowledge no child ever did receive a reply from his office.

What was sent to the school was this, from the Coal Division of the Department of Trade and Industry, along with two copies of the now infamous review, erroneously thought to be edifying to children whose families had already sussed the strategy.

Additionally, whilst in parliamentary terms the following may constitute an acceptable answer, since so many children had asked the Prime Minister direct questions it was taken as merely another acknowledgement of receipt when Eric Illsley, Member of Parliament for Barnsley Central, forwarded this to the school:

10 DOWNING STREET
LONDON SW1A 2AA

THE PRIME MINISTER

18 January 1993

Dear Eric,

Thank you for your letter of 10 December, enclosing some letters from pupils of the Willowgarth High School in Barnsley.

I have, in fact, already received some other letters from pupils at this school, through Norman Willis, and have written, through my Office, to thank them.

Yours sincerely,

John

Eric Illsley, Esq., M.P.

Clearly seeing the matter in the same light on the 22 October one twelve year old whose independent decision to take the matter to what he regarded as a higher authority; did receive a proper reply:

'From Buckingham Palace to the letter he had written to Her Majesty The Queen telling him that her Majesty appreciated the special place that miners had in the affections of so many people because of the difficult nature of their daily work. That she understood the effect of the pit closures on such tightly knit communities especially in a time of recession.

It pointed out that she was aware equally of the economic decisions her Ministers had to make regarding their energy policy. It also indicated that before final decisions were taken, the imposed moratorium on most of the closures enabled a review of the situation, to receive views from all concerned and to enable Parliament to debate the issue further. It closed by saying that The Queen was grateful that he had taken the trouble to write to her and it was most useful for her to have his views.'

Part 4:
A Book in a Day

It was the first day of their half-term holiday following an unsettled ending to a half term in thirty-one community schools. Despite that, over half the staff of Willowgarth High School as well as the Head, senior staff and governors, alongside an army of volunteers, agreed immediately to give up their Saturday 24 October 1992. Before the building of the new dual carriageway, the A628 ran straight through from Barnsley to Pontefract with just a minor loop down Engine Lane in Shafton through Grimethorpe with its rich seam of coal, to the neighbouring village of Brierley and back on to the A628. It led nowhere else! The political policy of closing thirty-one pits was feared by those coalfield communities to be taking them along a similar route – to nowhere. It seemed to those of us working in the school that 'The Road to Nowhere' was not only an appropriate title but an ironic expression of where the community felt it was going at that time. However, what began as the 'Road to Nowhere' and briefly became 'Supporting Grimethorpe' was finally published as *Energy is Coal*.

The day's writing was to begin at 6am on 24 October, and finish at 6pm for final editing and printing. At 6am the following day the book would be on the first coach to leave Grimethorpe for London for the biggest protest rally that Hyde Park had seen in many a year, if ever; nine million people with not a single arrest. Having agreed to take the first shift at exactly 6am I opened the visitors' book as the first walked through the door. We had hoped for a wide range of support but nothing could have prepared us for what happened or how demographically inclusive it would be. Staff and volunteers took on the job of reading through the messages including Michael Parkinson's contribution, to pull out the sections relevant to the pit and Parkinson senior, his dad Jack's memories of it. We had all contacted everyone we could think of asking for support but never estimated the response. Encouragement continued to stream in from the community, celebrities, BMBC Director of Education, and the Council, the MPs, and of course the National Union of Mineworkers, meaning there was just too much material to include in the space and time available for a book in a day. Half the staff of Willowgarth High School, a score from Yorkshire Arts Circus and Stan Barstow's team arrived to join an unprecedented Who's Who of supporters on the day between the last two dates in Dr Michael Clark's diary.

Saturday 24 October the day a book in a day was actually written. When the first shift started at 6am and supporters were signing in, the visitors' book records Rita Britton amongst the first through the door. She had been drumming up support across her networks in New York, Paris and Milan, so it was not really surprising to have her turn up with a message from the French Shoemakers' Federation saying that France and, in particular, the Federation, backed the British miners. Closely followed by husband Geoff and eldest son Mark, their accounts were some of the previously unused contributions now published here along with just a sample of others.

Rita's account was of an early childhood in a '2 up 2 down but I really loved that house. I used to get bathed in a tin bath in front of a lovely fire'. Quite typically in those days they lived as an extended family, her grandmother, her mother and her father and Rita. Granny Wilson was and remains her ideal of strength, individuality, enterprise and independence in a woman:

'She was a hard worker and a light sleeper, with an 18-hour-day which started as the local knocker-upper. She had a long stick tipped with a small piece of metal and she tapped on virtually every upstairs window in the neighbourhood to waken the day shift workers. She was also the one who brought their babies into the world, analysed their ailments, provided homespun remedies and finally laid them out when they died.'

Still alive in Rita's mind is hearing her grandmother talk of winters so cold and money so scarce that before she could bear to see them go out in freezing temperatures she would wrap her sons' legs in brown paper in the hope of keeping them a bit warmer before they went off to work down the pit. She recalls:

'I can still hear the comforting sound of clattering clogs as miners passed the house walking to and from work; and visual images of red eyes in black faces with teeth that looked whiter than anybody else had. They always seemed to have a sports jacket on that looked too small, stuck out at the back and they had their snap tins hanging from their belts.'

A later image she holds in her mind's eye is coming home from a party at 4am and driving past a line of miners, not standing but all crouching on their haunches waiting for the pit paddy to take them to work, it struck me that it was like seeing ghosts from the past. Re-asserting the community respect that miners traditionally earned in their closed communities, she contrasts the respect that also came naturally from them as she points out the one glaring error of *Brassed Off*, that in her whole life she never heard a miner use foul language. "Mild expletives yes, but they would never use obscenities in front of a woman or child; that was pit talk!"

One of Geoff Britton's first observations was also of rows of miners waiting for buses. Born locally into a mining family himself, as a child he still thought their ability to squat for long periods of time made them different in some way. It certainly may have been an indication of the muscles they developed working in 2 foot seams. Educational opportunities with scholarship places enabled him to go to Grammar School and take an alternative career path and he recalls the common feeling growing amongst miners' families in those days of improving education with its impact on rejection of the inbred routine career pattern; 'My lad's not going down pit!' He became an accountant; hence his own reason for supporting the campaign was based on economic logic as much as it was nostalgia or loyalty to his community:

'You have to support an industry to make it viable and it seems a strange thing to me that a local authority rips out solid fuel fires for more convenient forms of heating, at the same time as decrying the loss of the very industry which provides fuel for those fires. There is only one way to support the miners, and that is to buy their product.'

The young Mark Britton's support was less vocal but equally tangible; he watched, listened, questioned and then created the superb 12 feet high monochrome mosaic miners, created as flats for the latest production of *Children of the Dark* which were presented for display throughout the campaign and until Willowgarth High School finally closed.

The Rt Revd Bishop of Wakefield Nigel McCullough's own packed diary that Saturday was an indication of the demands on his time and workload. Prior professional commitments meant that he was unable to spend the whole day in the school but he was determined to show his support.

Arriving shortly after 6 30 with his seven-year-old daughter, and his driver Bob Seaton, both instantly asked if they could take part too and instantly did so.

Bishop Nigel's recollection is:

'It was soon after my arrival as Bishop of Wakefield that the Government announced its programme to close 31 collieries – amongst them was Grimethorpe. I remember well how devastating the news was to a community whose whole way of life had been centred on the pit.

Amidst the deep gloom that filled the people of this famous mining community, one bright ray of hope was Mel Dyke. With characteristic energy, imagination and perseverance she had galvanised young and old together and encouraged them to take pride in their memories and to look to the future. Her idea to get people to write down their thoughts to produce a book was a very important step in boosting morale by giving people some hope at a time of utter despair. I was there the day that book was written. It was a moving experience to hear and read people's stories – and I shall never forget the sense of value and purpose that was visibly restored among many people in Grimethorpe thanks to Mel.

I had been down a working mine myself; and I shared the anger and dismay that greeted the Government's determination to destroy the basis of people's lives especially in South and West Yorkshire.

I marched with the miners on several occasions behind the marvellous brass bands that for so long had been a part of our fabulous local culture. I spoke in Yorkshire and at Central Hall Westminster, at rallies on behalf of the threatened pit villages and I joined the courage Elizabeth Peacock, Conservative MP for Batley, who sacrificed her political career because of her stand against Government policy, in support of the miners and their families.

Elizabeth arranged for me to go with her to see Michael Heseltine, whose Government department was in charge of the closure programme. He was, actually, quite sympathetic, but obviously powerless to stand in the way of a determined and ruthless policy. We went into his office and he placed me in a low chair. He sat opposite me in a higher chair with the window behind him and the sun blazing into my eyes. An old trick! But my most treasured memory is of the journey we all made to London. The specially chartered train from Barnsley early on a winter's morning was packed. There was a subdued atmosphere underlain by a sense of genuine purpose: we were going to London to make our point about the wholly disgraceful and unfair manner in which the Government was treating communities whom, only a generation earlier, the nation had depended on in war. The rally and the handing in of a huge petition at 10 Downing Street for the Prime Minister were uplifting moments on a day that, for all the seriousness of its intention, was also an unforgettable adventure. At the end of it all, we got the special Barnsley train back home feeling weary, but glad we had made our mark – whatever the outcome might be.'

Too long for publication then, these letters dated 15 October and 17 October from Lady McGeogh must have been written as soon as she saw the news of the list of impending closures. Included now she would have doubtless ranked as a General or Commander of the unlikely force that mustered itself around pit villages during those days, weeks and months.

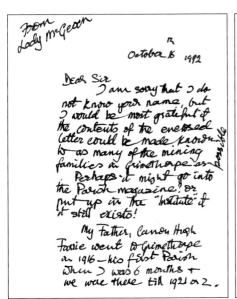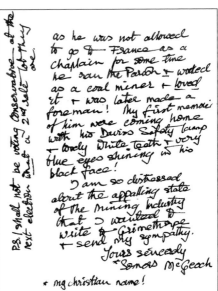

Letter from Lady McGeogh, sent to the miners of Grimethorpe.

Dear Miners of Grimethorpe

I and my family are so upset and angry at the terrible plight of so many thousands of miners all over the country that I felt I must write to the community of my early childhood and send my thoughts and great sympathy. I only trust that the strength of public opinion and the many Conservative rebels will cause the government to change its mind and unlike the Gadarene swine will stop at the edge of the precipice.

My Father was not allowed to go to the Front till nearly the end of the war but was sent to Grimethorpe as his first parish. He ran his parish but was also a miner and was made a foreman after a while; he said it was one of the happiest times of his life as he had a very good voice and he loved the large and excellent choir.

I was only five when we left but I remember the Institute and wandering around the village on my own and calling on my friends! I remember the Pickles and of course the Wards who all sang in the choir and May the eldest came with my parents when they left Grimethorpe and was with them for the rest of her life and was one of our family. They were 8 years in Roumania and seven years during the war in Malta and were starving for eighteen months and the bombing was appalling.

The ward family were; Mary, Stanley, Reggie, Hughie, Sidney, Edna, Douglas, Eileen and Albert. I am still in touch with Eileen's widower and Edna now very old. Marian Pickles went to America sometime after the 1918 war. I mention these friends in case anyone remembers them.

There was also a dear lady who used to take me out of church before the sermon when I was very small and used to read to me and feed a delicious Yorkshire pudding and gravy!

I have just heard that the famous Grimethorpe Band has done it again. Many congratulations!

This line comes with affectionate memories and deep sympathy and heartfelt good wishes for you all – miners and their families.

Yours sincerely
Somers McGeogh
PS
I fell in love with a young midshipman who is now a Vice Admiral and who was a submarine Captain in the last war and sank hundreds of thousands of tons of Rommell's oil supplies. We are now well passed our Golden Wedding – fifty-six years!

Part 4: A Book in a Day

In my book Stan Barstow is more like Broadband; a fast, direct and to the point channel of communication. I also think he invented Thora Hird! Well if he didn't, he definitely created Mrs Rothwell – the lovely Ingrid Rothwell's formidable mother in *A Kind of Loving* in which Thora warmed up for her later superbly snobbish Edie Pegden in Roy Clark's legendary *Last of the Summer Wine*. She never played a part badly in her life, but for me, along with one of Alan Bennett's greatest characters, Doris 'A Cream Cracker under the Settee' in the ever-watchable BBC series *Talking Heads*, they rank amongst the best roles she ever played. Anyone whoever read *Joby* at school will perhaps remember his perspective of a Northern childhood or recognise a familiar local characteristic long after scenes from *Twelfth Night* have faded. What I love about such writers is their ability to do that; to take a kitchen sink moment in time, a mundane or trivial incident and turn it into an unforgettable vignette. But Stan Barstow was not in that frame of mind that Saturday in October 1992, as he listened to the funny and sad, proud and humble stories that rolled in that day he wanted to tub thump and he did:

'All the men in my family were miners, my father, two grandfathers and several uncles; there's a solid backbone and grounding of mining in my life. Through my own observations of the area in which I was born and bred I have seen that although there may be many ways for a man to earn a living, the act of digging coal brings with it its own whole way of life out of which communities grow which without doubt are, big stabilisers on society.

Mrs Thatcher said that there is no such thing as society, a ludicrous statement, and one with which more and more people are taking issue. For years now we have been in danger of not just throwing away our manufacturing industry and the wealth connected with that, but the whole fabric of our society. There are people now who feel that they have nothing to give, that they have no place in the world around them; and this is a disgrace.

I am an author and I can think of a whole sweep of things, things which affect me and my environment. I hold to a strong belief that writers and artists have a duty to record these things, and I hope that I do that through my own novels.

I have become increasingly despondent as this mass shutdown seems to be devoid of any consideration of real people. The government is blinded by the false gods of profit and the marketplaces. As plain as the noses on our faces we are being led by, we are going down an illogical tunnel, and she dares to talk of "the enemy within".

We are in a situation where 60% of the population did not vote for the government we have and for a long period of time they have held absolute power; power to make irretrievable changes that have caused permanent damage.

The absence of any energy policy could leave us dependent on foreign nations for our fuel; coal imports, gas imports, oil imports. To throw away national assets like this is going to leave us with no purpose in life. It is all very well to have a service industry, a leisure industry and the arts, but they cannot exist without a vehicle to create wealth. We have to have our own energy; we have to create that wealth. We will be nothing without coal.'

What I like even more about teacher-people like Stan is that they can also get others to write above and beyond their belief in their own ability. I saw him and others do that all that day. Not only did they write of his own life and fears, but sat with, coaxed, listened to, heard and scribed for people who felt they would never be able to put their feelings on paper, and then they did.

Elizabeth North took an early and unusual backseat not just writing her own views but listening to others tell their tales, and in her own meticulous handwriting set down their thoughts. Sheila Salt, wife of the man who as Chair of the Coalfields Community Campaign (CCC) would follow the day up by organising the CCC Christmas Carol Service in Westminster Abbey less than a month later and Leader of Barnsley Council told her, 'My family's been alright so far. My husband's in insurance and I work with mentally handicapped adults.'

Interestingly the 'so far' indicated that their relatively safe situation was potentially, if not probably, only a present tense factor. People who felt totally secure in those dark days were few and far between, and the predictable fall out from the decimation of the country's biggest industry was in clear view in thirty-one villages that day, if not in Westminster.

'There was a fear that free school lunches were going to be cut. That meant sandwiches for kids at lunchtime and for some that had been the only hot meal they'd get. Like many other women here I worked in a food kitchen during the strike. I remember one little girl who

Team work: Author Stan Barstow, centre, and colleagues Steve Davenport, left, and Ian Daley who helped produce a history of Grimethorpe colliery in one day's work. Picture: Chris Lawton.

Villagers unite to record the past glory of colliery without a future

Keith Bunker

VILLAGERS "closed the book" on their doomed pit at the weekend.

Writers, editors and illustrators from across Yorkshire — among them author Stan Barstow — combined their talents to record the story of Grimethorpe colliery, near Barnsley, in a single day.

Organiser Mel Dyke said the idea was to put down on paper the 99-year history of the pit before it becomes a victim of the Government's fiercely-criticised closure programme.

Grimethorpe is one of those which failed to win a reprieve, and will close next week with the loss of 950 jobs.

The project was co-ordinated by Yorkshire Art Circus at the request of teachers and pupils from the village's Willowgarth High School.

Local people were asked to recall their memories of the pit to a team of writers, who worked throughout Saturday and eventually collated more than 18,000 words.

Among those who contributed pre-written pieces were South Yorkshire celebrities Michael Parkinson and Brian Blessed.

Mrs Dyke, deputy head at Willowgarth, said: "The response was unbelievable — it really was so heartening.

"People from across the spectrum contributed. There were wonderful rolling stories and words that were acid, cynical, resentful.

"Whatever the outcome we have given something positive and not destructive. We have caught a moment in the life and death of a great little mining village."

The book, *Energy For Coal*, was put together in a photocopied form and it is hoped to have it published and on sale by Wednesday.

Yorkshire Art Circus spokesman Brian Lewis said: "We could have gone anywhere but we chose Grimethorpe because the school asked us to help and because the colliery band once did us a big favour.

"We are all shocked by the short-term view the Government seems to it appears to have underestimated the effect closure will have on social and community life in this region.

"The best way we can respond in these circumstances was to put our skills at the service of this community."

Photo and article by kind permission of Chris Lawton, Keith Bunker and *The Yorkshire Post*.

came in with her father at around 11am one day asking for her dinner because she hadn't eaten since 7am that day, we were still cooking to start serving at 12. We'd get potatoes and vegetables, given by a local shop, and the local Chip Shop would peel them for us and the Lyons factory nearby donated cakes to serve as a sweet. Everybody did everything they could for everybody else. I used to take some of our clothes to miners' families once including a coat of my daughter's which fit a miner's wife. She had a little girl who waiting for me said, "Mrs. Salt, please can you fetch me a coat next week?"'

Joan Peach recalled:

'I had a hairdressing business during the 3-day week period in the early 70s which was badly affected by that situation. Everyone went home with their hair in rollers when the electricity went off. They'd dry their hair at home and then come back when the power came back on. People just got on with it; the landlord had a bread shop underneath my salon and used to take sandwiches down to the miners made from bread that was left over.'

Her father, grandfathers and great-grandfathers on both sides of the family had a link going back to 1908, all working in Grimethorpe pit. With the phlegmatic characteristic acceptance of such routine risk in the line of duty that mining communities share with military families, she explained:

'I had an uncle who was killed in the pit; my grandad lost a leg and my great -grandad was also killed underground – all in this same pit. I feel so angry now as I look back over my family's involvement in mining here and realise that now there will be no-one left who is directly concerned in mining.'

Acting Director of Education, Malcolm Warrington, had first come to the area in 1990 and been involved in that year's reorganisation of the Willowgarth pyramid:

'The 1991 Budget was particularly severe but within the Council there has always been a feeling of trying to do the best for this community where there are consistently high levels of children receiving free schools meals, and to benefit it as much as is possible. The Education Department has tried to deliver Scheme of Aid efficiently and the area is benefiting from City Challenge 2 funding. As there has always been a high take-up of use, there has always been a library presence in Grimethorpe too. The work done here in Community Education, run by Jack Peach, not only delivers basic adult education in literacy and numeracy, but also Community development projects. During the Miners' strike, Trevor Brooks the Chief Education Officer was welcomed in Grimethorpe schools on a regular basis. There is a partnership of Education with other statutory and voluntary groups such as NACRO. The Rev, Tony McPherson is a co-opted member on the Education Committee and so can represent the Church's views there. There is a strong feeling that everyone is interested in the welfare of the community here.'

He was correct in that and in ensuring that the Church was represented there.

Vice Chair of Governors Amelia Bailey looked back to the 1920s and recalled:

'Grimethorpe Colliery provided me with one of the highlights of my childhood – and there were not many of those in the 1920s and 1930s! I was privileged to be taken on a visit down the pit. We went one lovely Sunday morning during the August holiday dressed in the oldest clothes we had, we didn't have many at all. We were first taken to the engine room and allowed to pull the lever which let the cage down to the bottom of the pit. Then we were taken down in this cage, not a quick drop which the young lads when they first started working at the pit used to dread. What a lovely experience to see the pit ponies in their whitewashed stalls with their name plates over the doors. Of course this part of the pit was well lit, but then we went on to see the places where our brothers, fathers and uncles worked, lovely for a few hours' visit but afterwards we realised how awful it was for the men who had to stay down there digging coal and so for 8 hours every day.'

Headteacher Tony Dorney had particular praise for the band in one of his contributions:

'I am proud to be headteacher of Willowgarth High School in. One of my reasons for coming to Grimethorpe was the Band. They are quite simply the best brass band in the world. It has been an immense privilege over the years to let them use the school hall to rehearse for big competitions in concert hall conditions. The threat to the Band through closure of Grimethorpe pit touches me deeply and I desperately wanted them to win the national championships again at what could perhaps be their last chance. I could have wept for joy when I heard that they had won; I do hope that the Band will survive and continue to give so much pleasure to so many.'

He had his wish and twenty years later though struggling still there is again renewed hope for the Band's survival.

Despite enormous worldwide support to save the viable pit that fate was already sealed in 1992 and in 1993 it was bricked up and shut as planned.

A book in a day, however, survived.

Published by Willowgarth School, Grimethorpe and Yorkshire Art Circus, Glasshoughton, Castleford.

Editors
Reini Schuhle, Barbara Clayton, Liz Cashdan

Editorial support team
Ann Cross, Pam Davenport, Steve Davenport, Ian Daley, Mel Dyke, Brian Lewis, Tony Lumb, Liz Lloyd, Linda Malkin, Harry Malkin, Linda McGillivray, Liz North, Pam Oxley, Joan Thornton, Mick Wilson.

Photographs:	Steve McClarence
Book Design:	Brian Lewis and Tony Lumb
Cover Design:	Harry Malkin and Steven Atkinson
Cover Illustration:	Harry Malkin
Printing:	E Atkinson and Sons. Printers Pontefract.

YORKSHIRE ART CIRCUS

Yorkshire Art Circus is a unique book publisher. We work to increase access to writing and publishing and to develop new models of practice for arts in the community.
Yorkshire Art Circus believes that everyone has a story to tell and devises innovative ways to bring new writers to new audiences.
For details about our complete programme of work contact us at: Yorkshire Art Circus, School Lane, Glass Houghton, Castleford, West Yorkshire WF10 4QH. Telephone (0977) 550401.

WILLOWGARTH SCHOOL

As part of Barnsley MBC, Willowgarth High School is the community school for the mining village of Grimethorpe. This book is our way of giving our community a voice at a most difficult time in its history.

We would like to thank the people who have contributed to this book:-

David Aitchison, Dave Ardron, Judith Ardron, Phillip Ardron, Cath Badrock, Julie Bagshaw, Audrey Bailey, Amelia Bailey, Chris Baines, Carol Bamforth, Connie Barstow, Stan Barstow, William Bates, Barbara Bennett, Harry Blower, Sophie Booth, Arthur Bradbury, Graham Bratley, Max Bristowe, Geff Brittan, Rita Brittan, Rebecca Brookes, Mrs K Brown, Tom Brown, Tommy Butterworth, Mr Carr, Doreen Cauldwell, Jane and Michael Caulfield, Alexander Clayton, Ian Clayton, Neil Clarkson, Robert Clegg, Susan Clegg, David Clark, Roy Cuthbert, Sharon Chamberlain, Nigel O'Callaghan, Pat Doyle, John Dawson, A Dorney, Janet Dalton, Mrs Dixon, Pete Dixon, W Denton, Lesley Darbyshire, Jean Eels, Kevin Eland, Ginette Eddy, Helen Fenton, Robert Foster, Margaret Ferry, Mr & Mrs J K Fearn, Claire & Philip Geeson, Sandra Geeson, Noel Green, Michael Green, Rebecca Hanson, Andrew Holmes, Henry Hall, Edward Hibbert, Madge Hutchinson, Ron & Georgina Hooley, Tommy Hibbert, Ann Harrett, Maggie Harper, Rebecca Harrison, Mike Hill, Keeley Hull, Jeff Hyde, Matthew Hancock, Eric Howard, Neil Horbury, Irene Heron, Vicky Hulme, Sharon Hancock, Ken Hirst, Ken Hancock, David Harnett, Anne Harnett, Lynn Haywood, Michael Heard, Gail Hancock, Eric Illsley, Edna Johnson, Angela Johnson, Geoffrey King, Barbara Kenworthy, Caren Kaye, Alwyn Kaye, Mary King, Brian Kaye, Julie Kearford, Fred Kennedy, Eddy Leyland, Dennis Lawley, Liz Lloyd, Jack Laycock, Melvyn Leonard, Eric Leese, Betty Makings, Roy Mason, Mr Middleton, Tony McPherson, Philip Milner, Cheryl McLaran, Julie Mitchell, Somers McGeoch, Sheena McClure, Kay Marrison, Elizabeth North, Martin Oxley, Julie Pilsworth, Terry Patchett, Heather Parkinson, Jack & Joan Peach, Michael Parkinson, Robert Porter, Emma Rollinson, Beverley Rossi, Derek Robinson, Jim Seston, Carol Sykes, Ellen Smith, Hugo Smith, Mr Smith, Brian Smith, Caroline Salt, Sheila Salt, Kenneth Stanley, Kim Swift, Robert Scothern, Hedley Salt, Richard Shepherd, Gary Smith, David Swift, Paul Spialek, Kenneth Taylor, Christine Taylor, Joan Thornton, Peter Tait, M.Tayler, Phil Thompson, Kevin Taylor, Brian Thompson, Peter Thompson, Tashy, Sam Tascks, Colin Tindall, Alex Vodden, Geoff Vodden, Tony Waltham, Arthur Whittaker, Sylvia Wilson, Ron Wilby, Florence Whittlestone, Mr Wardle, David Wiley, Stephen Wood, Steven Wood, Johnny Wood, Malcolm Warrington, Alan Young.

Chapter 5

Scottish Miners' March
November 1992

By the start of November things were settling back into normal routine and there was a slight feeling of aftermath about the place. Pockets of opportunity and optimism cropped up here and there and the youngsters found new incentives on which to focus. Radio 1FM set up a competition for schools to win a computer which created so much interest a design was chosen and entered by the school.

We were unlucky with that one, but towards the end of the month news came that a group of twelve Scottish miners including the President of the Scottish NUM was to march 646 miles from Glasgow to London to protest against the pit closures. Far more than twice the 246 miles of the 1936 Jarrow March later to be immortalised by Alan Price's 1974 *Jarrow Song* hit, but its purpose was not dissimilar. The Geordie Boys' had been to highlight the collapse of industry on Tyneside in 1936; The Scots' reason was to highlight the decimation of the coal industry in 1992 so of course was a subject of intense local interest.

When the itinerary was announced indicating that Grimethorpe pit yard was to be on the route there was great interest which bubbled over into excitement when the next big news came – that they were going to detour from the planned route not only to come through Grimethorpe, but to actually march through the school with the banner. Until recently, when recognition of our returning soldiers was again given that public status, you would have had to be from an area where marches are inherently a part of pride and history to understand what that meant.

All we knew was that the march would be led in by a piper and that as many children as could be gathered together would be able to watch. We wanted to welcome the visitors properly of course, but with as little disruption to classes throughout the morning as possible. The dining hall held was big

WE WROTE A BOOK IN A DAY
TO FIGHT GRIMETHORPE'S PIT CLOSURE
WE NEED OUR OWN COMPUTER TO
RECORD AND CONTINUE OUR CAMPAIGN

Radio1 FM Competition Willowgarth's entry form.

enough to hold over two entire year groups and other rooms and corridors gave additional good viewing opportunities. On the day itself the leaders of the march were in touch with the school office through the police escort, reporting their progress and estimated time of arrival at the school.

When they were reported to be approaching the next village the children were assembled and what seemed like a long wait began. Inevitably their excitement led to chatter which drowned out any prospect of the hearing the approach. Childhood memories of old club trips came to mind when the first child to spot Blackpool tower was the star of the day; and modern youth was equally conned into quietness and re-directed into who would be the first one to hear the sound of the bagpipes. When the men turned into the school drive the skirl of the pipes broke into the sound of silence. When the big doors were then swung open the eruption of noise was unbelievable and as one boy reminded me many years later:

'I know I have never heard a cheer like it, except when Barnsley went up into Premier League. It just blew everybody away.'

Increasingly any ingrained reluctance which can block some youngsters from making any written contribution, even in a school with as strong a tradition of good teaching of English as Willowgarth seemed to fade as whole sets of children routinely recorded their feelings in words or pictures, drama, music and dance. Whilst some of the most articulate were ready, willing and able to undertake interviews with newspaper and TV journalists, and did, even children previously hindered by their perception of their own ability, or lack of it, seemed to lose that concern in a new tidal wave of enthusiasm to be a part of it. Suddenly it became cool to be involved and any lack of confidence dissolved.

In these accounts of the day, these two boys' writing takes first place as it was to my knowledge the only written work they had ever asked to do:

'We were all lined up, Chris, Lee, Andrew and another year 7 lad held the doors open for the miners. When the miners marched down the corridor there was a big cheer and people gave the miners bars of chocolate and miners gave people stickers then some people came down with banners. It was a very happy thing for me to see the miners marching, I thought it was a moving experience for me and the atmosphere was brilliant and very exciting.

At the march I was there. There was half of Willowgarth waiting for the moment of history. I was so proud of the miners walk through our school, from Scotland they were walking 600 and odd miles. One of them was crying and Matron went up to the miners and said do you want some plasters for your feet. The miner said I'm ok love, it's the cheering. It's the best moment of my life thanks. It was the best moment of my life as well and to be on TV. I will be in History now. It is good to know the Scottish miners did the march. When I am older I will tell my grandchildren and make them proud.'

For others their place in any pecking order was irrelevant; they simply wanted to be a part of it. It was that sense of unity, caring and sharing pride that some would have to wait another twenty years until the Queen's Golden Jubilee and the 2012 London Olympics to feel again:

'It was a normal playtime but we were in the Library being told we were going to be part of a march, the Scottish Miners' March. The march started from Scotland and was going to London because of the pit closures in Scotland. Our pit closures were getting a lot more coverage than the Scottish but they were going to change it. About twenty miners were coming through the school and we were there to cheer them on. As soon as they were sighted silence fell on the piper and the sound of trumpets filled the cold morning air like an arrow leading them to the school. The first cheer was amazing. It filled the school with a glow that was indescribable. We put chocolates in their buckets to satisfy their needs and in return we got a sheet of stickers. After when all the miners had gone through we heard that one of the miners had shed a tear because of all the cheering. It will be a day I will never forget.

The miners came to Willowgarth and years 8 and 7 and all the teachers came out into the Dinner Hall and all year 8 and 7 gave them bars of chocolate then they went outside to interview some of the pupils. Afterwards they went to the stute*and had something to eat then they went down to the pit and then to Barnsley and they left there hoping the pit never had to close and I felt very touched. I felt very sorry for the miners.

As the Scottish miners approached the doors of the school all fell silent, then the doors were opened and a giant cheer was given off as the miners walked through the corridor, it was brilliant! I have never felt like I felt that morning in my entire life. The atmosphere was electric, for those few moments as the miners walked through the corridor I didn't seem myself, I didn't seem to care about trivial things anymore like what hair styles my friends have and whether or not it was pocket money day, but for those few minutes all I felt was a mixture of emotions towards the miners who were courageously marching 600 miles to save the coal mining industry. The thing that struck me was that they weren't just doing it for themselves but for everyone.

---

* *Stute* – local Working Men's Club & Institute

When the Scottish miners came in I felt proud of them and I felt excellent myself. I know I felt very sorry for them, but I would not walk 200 miles. They had blisters on their feet and bad legs, and they've got to march another 200 miles or more. I don't know how they do it. I just hope the best for them. When they got into Grimethorpe they walked into the school gates and the band played Jerusalem and when they walked through the door there was such a cheer if you'd had a glass cup it would have gone smash. But unfortunately we didn't. Some of the miners were crying. The matron asked one of the miners if he wanted some plasters but the miner said "NO, after that – I am walking on thin air".'

Rita Poole was the School Matron and along with Laboratory Technician Linda Jackson had taken on responsibility for putting Deputy Head Roger Beswick's latest marathon timetable conversion into smooth running practice. Her own memories of that day were as strong as ever twenty years later. 'It was hard not to feel down sometimes, but so much of what we did with the children in school was really fun, especially some of their comments when we were setting the balloons off, they had us in stitches with helium and they just loved it. There were sad days, but then it was absolutely uplifting at times!' She was close to tears describing the day of the march, how 'the children had been so quiet then the roof almost went when that cheer went up! The noise was quite unprecedented and seeing such strong men like them in tears was new to us all. People thought they were just tough guys but that day showed what they were really going through. I knew even before he said it that it was emotional pain bringing that response from the young miner – not the blisters on his feet!' She knew well enough, from her own family's experience of receiving 'strike bags' from her mother every week with what they described as essential luxuries, such as butter and toilet rolls and the only heating in the house coming from one coal fire on which they would burn any and everything.

The children's accounts continue:

'When the music started up outside everybody was excited. Then the Scottish Miners appeared in the doorway and the roar and encouragement we gave them was like magic. I felt grateful, happy and sad all at the same time. I was grateful that they had come to see us and out school. I was happy to be part of Willowgarth's support and happy and proud that they had come to see us. But amongst the happiness and magic I was sad, that the miners weren't here for pleasure, but here passing on their way to London to save their jobs and an industry. I was moved again afterwards when Mrs Dyke told us how they wanted to come back through and how they cried because of the encouragement we gave them and all the other miners. During their walk though the school we gave the miners chocolate and they brought the Grimethorpe Colliery banner though which has never been in any school before. I was very happy and I really hope they keep their jobs and save the coal industry.

On the 30.11.92 the group from Scotland came on a march to try and save theirs and other people's jobs. I was at the front (holding the door) when the first people came in and all the teachers and pupils from Willowgarth High gave a big cheer it was brilliant just standing there and watching them go by. When the last lot came in they had a big banner with them and that brought the biggest cheer of all. They deserve a medal for marching to Willowgarth at least and they are still going on to march to London. So they will have marched 400 miles by the time they get to London. I felt so grateful that they have gone through this. It was just brilliant to see the looks on their faces. Some were even crying. They are worth anything. I would give them my last penny for this.

We gave them a warm and hopefully memorable welcome by giving them a standing ovation which despite the weather made them smile and even moved some of the men to tears. I felt proud to be witness to such emotion. Even though it was a cold, wet day the men had the guts and courage to keep marching to protest against something which they and many more people know is wrong. Even though it was only a short visit through our school it made a difference to all of us because it gave us a chance to show our appreciation for what they were trying to do to help the mining communities all over Britain. It made me feel proud because they had the will power to keep going and not to give up. It also gave us all something to remember and talk about for a long time to come. It is incredible that such a small group of people brought and I hope took away so much. Well done lads keep the effort up!

The Scottish miners' march was one of the most moving things that I had ever experienced. We could hear a piper as they came over the hill on their way to Willowgarth High School. I stood in the corridor to give them a cheer on their way past. Then they came through the door and all of a sudden there was an enormous roar of children, clapping, whistling and shouting as the miners limped through the corridor. The applause never stopped, and then the noise just boomed as Grimethorpe Colliery banner came through. One of the younger miners was drawn to tears as he walked through the crowd. The emotion was the most tremendous I have ever felt in my entire life. I could have cried tears of joy and sadness because it was so amazing, what people will do just to help others who need it. Afterwards the press interviewed some of the children, and then the miners marched out of the school towards Grimethorpe where they had their dinner before marching onto Barnsley. It was an occasion that I will remember for the rest of my life because if how much it meant to millions of people – and I was there to witness it. It was amazing.'

Nine of the men made it for Christmas arriving in London on Saturday 19 December 1992. Their families who were flown from Glasgow the day before and greeted by members of the airport's trade unions joined their men at Congress House for a formal reception compared by top DJ John Peel.

The TUC issued a national request that at 8pm on Saturday 19 December 1992 all lights in London be switched off for five minutes as silent recognition of the protest. Nationwide other areas joined in; and you couldn't see a hand in front of your face in Yorkshire!

On 21 December the High Court issued two rulings:

1 – That that the Government's decision to close thirty-one pits was unlawful.
2 – That the decision to close ten pits and to place twenty-one pits under review was also unlawful.

And then it was Christmas.

Chapter 6

Westminster Abbey Children's Carol Service

The Coalfields' Community Campaign organised a Christmas Carol Service in Westminster Abbey on 17 December 1992. From each of the other thirty blighted communities an equal number of miners' children were chosen to represent their school and their colliery. Along with those young representatives in recognition of the unique battle which that community continued to fight, hundreds of children from Grimethorpe were invited to attend. Staffed by teachers and volunteers the convoy of coaches left in the dark to follow the line through then still visible pit areas of West and South Yorkshire, Derbyshire, Nottinghamshire and Leicestershire. Bubbling children doing map traces and quizzes waved back as traffic on both sides of the M1 sounded horns or gave thumbs up recognition.

A strong memory is of the stillness that cut through that as the twin pit heads of shafts standing side by side at Markham Main were pointed out, resembling a cenotaph to the memory of the eighteen men killed in 1973 when the cage broke loose and fell to the bottom.

Progress was good, uneventful feeding and watering with punctual returns to the fleet of coaches meant we arrived in London in good time. We had no forewarning that Baker Street would bring a serious delay due to a reported bomb scare; so it was with increasing concern that we edged into Parliament Square for the 1 30 start of the event to see Big Ben's familiar face showing the time as 1 37pm. I was desperately trying to think of a way to sneak 700 plus children into a church service which had already begun without creating chaos when the familiar figure of Norman Willis standing in front of the great West door moved forward. Fearful of the predictable reply I asked if we were too late, his grin said it first followed by, 'No; we've just asked them to play some more carols, we're not starting without the Grimethorpe kids!'

Photograph by kind permission of Linda McAvan MEP, Yorkshire and The Humber.

Linda McAvan, Labour MEP for Yorkshire and The Humber recalls:

'In autumn 1992 I was working as European Officer at the Coalfield Communities Campaign (CCC), a small organisation based in Barnsley which looked after the interests of local authorities in our mining communities. Those of us close to the coal industry were not surprised when

John Major's government announced a major closure programme of thirty-one of the country's mines. In the run-up to the April general election, we had been warning that the Tories were determined to finish off what Margaret Thatcher had started by closing much of what was left of the coal industry – and privatise the rest. But what did take us aback was the scale of the public outrage at the government's announcement, not just in the North, Scotland and Wales where you might have been expected it, but right across the country. There were huge demonstrations in London and across the country, women from the home counties vented their anger on the *Jimmy Young Show* and other radio phone ins and we were inundated with TV stations wanting to meet 'real' miners and their families for their stories of trouble up north. The public mood was clearly shifting away from the 'enemy within' culture of the 80s and for a brief period, it seemed possible that we might actually stop the closures.

That optimism started to evaporate by late autumn. The government had seen off a potential backbench rebellion by launching an enquiry into the closures, gambling that by buying time, the miners' story would disappear off the front page. Which of course it did, so one afternoon at the CCC offices in Barnsley, we started to wonder how we could recapture the public imagination, get the miners back up the political agenda. A germ of an idea began to form in our minds. Christmas was coming. Could we organise some kind of Christmas appeal for the mining communities of Britain? Launch it with children singing Christmas carols in different communities, or better still in London near Westminster?

Looking back, it is hard now to remember exactly how we got to the idea of a carol concert in Westminster Abbey on the last day before Parliament rose for the Christmas recess. But central to the idea becoming a reality were Barbara Edwards, then Deputy Director or the CCC, the late Hedley Salt, highly respected Barnsley Council leader and Chair of CCC and Nigel McCulloch, then Bishop of Wakefield.

I think I am safe to say that none of us really thought the event would be as big or as emotional as it turned out to be. I will never forget the sight of coach after coach arriving in Whitehall, bringing the children from the mining communities who had travelled long hours, some through the night, to get to London. They were so excited and yet fell quiet when ushered into Westminster Abbey to be greeted by the music of the Grimethorpe Colliery Band. It could have been a scene in a film and for me, somehow foreshadows that famous Albert Hall scene in *Brassed Off*, though our children were the genuine article not characters from the fictional Grimley.

The special job I had been given that day was to get thirty-one children, one from each of the mining communities whose pits were due for closure, to Downing Street to present a Christmas card to John Major urging him to think again. We had seated the thirty-one children together in the Abbey so that we could get them out first at the end of the service. Just before we left, a journalist from the BBC asked to speak to one of the children live on air. One young girl volunteered. I don't remember her name but I do remember what she said. Asked by the journalist what she would like for Christmas, the girl replied "I just want my Daddy to keep his job". No prompting. No rehearsals, but enough to bring a tear to the eye of the journalists and those listening in that day. Did her wish come true? I doubt it, unless he was one of the few lucky enough to get deployed to one of the few remaining pits. Yes we made headline news that day. We had wall to wall coverage on local TV and radio. We made *John Craven's Newsround*. But the Prime Minister did not open the door of No 10 to the children from the coalfields. Instead we left the card with the policeman on duty. I can't remember whether we ever got an acknowledgement from No 10. In the New Year, the pits were closed and the rest, as they say, is history.'

Barbara Edwards [Deputy Director, Coalfield Communities campaign at the time].
Her own account of that event:

'17 December 1992 – a scarcely believable day. The Coalfield Communities Campaign orchestrated an event that was to be a focus for the nationwide, grassroots protest against Michael Heseltine's intention to close thirty-one coal mines.

A conference in Parliament headed up by top politicians from all parties and church leaders from all the major denominations would be the precursor to a unique and unprecedented event at nearby Westminster Abbey.

Over 1500 schoolchildren from all thirty-one communities threatened by the closures packed this great historic church next to the heart of government for a Carol Service to show peacefully (and joyfully) to those in power the importance of these pits for their own future and the future wellbeing of their towns and villages.

My own memories of the day are many but for me, despite the underlying seriousness of the event, there were several little cameos that embodied the specialness of the occasion and that still move me to this day:

Entering the Abbey alone and hours before the start of the Carol Service to be met by the magnificent and powerful sound of world renowned Grimethorpe Colliery Band rehearsing *O come all ye faithful*.

A coach pulling up outside the Abbey packed full of children with each and every window festooned with homemade SAVE OUR PIT bunting. The children from Seaham, County Durham had made a 6/7 hour journey that morning. Most had never been to London.

Press and media interest was enormous. All the national press, TV and radio were there (including *Blue Peter*!). But it was quite special to overhear a hard-nosed TV man gently asking a shy young girl if she would like to use his phone to tell her parents that she would shortly be on TV so that they would have time to tune in.

The events of that day were intended to highlight the anger and strength of feeling not only in these thirty-one communities but throughout the UK. Conservative Associations countrywide, even from Surrey, contacted the CCC sharing their concerns. Clearly, Michael Heseltine had misjudged the mood of the nation but in the end his political skills saved his day. He played a long game and set up a Government review of the coal industry which took months to complete. When the report was finally published the public anger had inevitably abated and the issue cooled. In the end he and Maggie got their way and Britain's coal industry was all but destroyed.'

For Ron Blackburn, Head of Lower School at Willowgarth High School the day was an extra special one:

'17 December 1992 was the day of the Coalfields Communities Campaign's Christmas Carol Service at Westminster Abbey. It was also my 50th birthday. It was most appropriate that I should spend this special day surrounded by miners' families and their supporters as my father, grandfather, uncles and many friends were miners for all of their lives. My own son was able to be present in the Abbey that day to celebrate both events.

My father began work when he was thirteen years old at Barrow Colliery and stayed there for all of his working career, retiring as a colliery overman in 1982. His brother, my Uncle Sid, was awarded the Edward Medal (later converted to the George Cross) for bravery in the 1947 Barnsley Main Colliery Disaster. Grandad was in charge of the pithead baths at Barrow Colliery and all of his four sons worked in the pits. I spent the whole of my teaching career in mining areas – Hatfield, Worsbrough and Grimethorpe, so I felt at home in the midst of that mining fraternity – but the fact that it was in Westminster Abbey was amazing!

It was a dull, dismal, foggy start to the day and we were not sure we would arrive at the Abbey in time because of the weather. I don't think the children were too concerned about that as they were tucking into the sandwiches, cakes, sweets and pop that had been so generously provided by their parents, despite the hardships they were suffering at the time. To their children the trip was a holiday.

The grandeur of the Abbey was a different world for all of us. The organ itself must have been the size of ten Yorkshire Traction buses, and its height seemed to go forever. Following the service our pupils were invited to a tour of the building and appeared to take everything in their stride and made every effort to befriend the Abbey staff there to ensure that everything ran smoothly. They seemed quite taken with our children and engaged in quiet conversations with several in small groups. They were most patient and helpful, even when lighted candles were blown out by some of our more playful pupils singing happy birthday – and to their credit they did see the funny side of this.

The funniest moment that lives with me still happened on our way back to the buses. Walking in pairs along Whitehall we were behind another school walking in single file with a teacher at the front and another bringing up the rear. An unsuspecting member of the public walking alongside this group went down an underpass that led to toilets and the other side of Whitehall, and of course the inevitable happened, as one of their pupils innocently followed on so did the rest of the class. A minute or two later we passed the lead teacher with the rest of his class frantically trying to ascertain the whereabouts of the rest of his group. It didn't help when our children merrily informed him of the disappearing act adding that by then they were all probably locked up in the Tower of London!

It was a long tiring day and the children on our bus soon sang themselves to sleep that day, but often recalled the experience as long as they were in school. For me, I still have to pinch myself when I think back and remember that I spent my 50th birthday surrounded by a hundreds of members of a mining fraternity in Westminster Abbey. Not only that – I was serenaded by the world champions – Grimethorpe Colliery Band and blessed by Bishop Nigel of Wakefield!'

From the Coalfields Community Campaign video of the service with Bishop Nigel's recollection:

Bishop Nigel's unescorted dash to the pulpit of Westminster Abbey! Image by kind permission of Coalfield Regeneration Trust

'For me, and I think for many, a special highlight of the day was the specially-arranged service in Westminster Abbey. We were nearing Christmas and so Tony Macpherson (the excellent vicar of Grimethorpe – wearing as ever his distinctive black beret) and Ian Gaskill (a key member of my clergy whose amazing contribution to enable all this to happen all this was outstanding) got the Abbey to agree to a special Carol Service accompanied by the brilliant and famous Grimethorpe Colliery Band. My job was to preach.

As we got near to the start of the service (and once we had persuaded the authorities to allow the band to play from the very spot where our kings and queens are crowned – rather than the original plan of hiding them in the organ loft), the buzz of excitement was rising. Every seat was taken chiefly by school pupils from each of the thirty-one threatened pit villages. Meanwhile in the vestry the procession of senior clergy was solemnly forming up. It was at that point that I mentioned to the Dean and his senior staff that, with so many young people present, I was concerned that the architecture of the Abbey meant that those seated in the main nave of the building would be unable to see what was happening.

So I said that halfway through my address I would move from the pulpit and go down, through the choir stalls to the nave, to speak to and to be seen by everyone there. At this point I was told that a verger would slowly lead me down. But I protested that would not fit in to how I wanted to do it, and it would look so pompous. The reply was stern: "no-one taking part in a service here moves without being verged". I thought to myself: well that tradition is about to end!

Everyone enjoyed the carols accompanied by our colliery band and then we came to my sermon. I went up into the pulpit wearing a miner's hard hat which I had been lent on the train and dared to wear it: so I did. It fitted the theme I was planning to take – which was to tell the story of Jesus by using the letters M I N E R, starting with Mary at the birth of Christmas. After reaching N for Nazareth, I decided it was time to move an eagle-eyed verger immediately noted my body language and started to get up. Instantly I rushed down the pulpit steps and ran through the choir, got to the nave-and then carried on the sermon presumably leaving an astonished verger behind! It meant that everyone in the Abbey felt included and silly pomposity was avoided. I though I'd never be invited into the Abbey again. But some years later the Dean, in an autobiographical reflection, mentioned the occasion including my preaching wearing the miner's helmet and describing what I had done as one of the few gimmicks he had seen in a Church that had actually worked. And I was invited back!'

Dr Tony Dorney and Bishop Nigel leading the thirty-one children to Downing Street.
Coalfield Communities Campaign

Chapter 7

'An Evening of Mining History in Words and Music'

With a very different Christmas for most, and few believing that the ninety-day reprieve would be anything more than that, the New Year of 1993 began with increased resolution and a cross-curricular project involving virtually the whole school with a heartening range of support from 'outsiders'.

The announcement that the school's dramatic production would take place on Wednesday 27 January initially brought such a great demand for tickets that a second night had to be added. Hot on the heels of the massive interest and support for the Scottish miners' visit, the school hall was no longer big enough and Barnsley Civic Hall was instantly sold out. As word of mouth spread the word there was a waiting list which could have filled the biggest venue in the town for a week and it was the hottest ticket in town.

Part one of the evening was a performance of *Children of the Dark*.

Tucked away in that cast list was one child's name which twenty years later would be making headlines at the Edinburgh Festival. Gary Clark first left Willowgarth to go on to Barnsley College where he decided he was better suited to dance than drama. But more of Gary later!

Having already been a volunteer and contributor to a book in a day, Art undergrad Mark Britton turned up trumps again, working flat out to create the 12 feet high portraits to be used as scenery in the production. As the program said, the school was 'greatly indebted to him for his willingness to devote his time, talent and enthusiasm for the production at such very short notice.' It was even more grateful to accept his offer of loaning the paintings for display in the school. They were formally unveiled there in unison by the Mayors of Barnsley and Brierley on the occasion of Rodney Bickerstaffe's final visit to the school to present awards

112

*Paintings by kind permission of Mark Britton used as staging
flats for the 1993 Willowgarth public performance of* Children
of the Dark. Photograph by kind permission of John Britton

to high achieving students, and remained there in pride of place until
Willowgarth High School closed.

The interval was a buzz of excitement and enthusiasm for the children
most of whom had never appeared in such a grand public venue before.
Ironically the one boy born in the catchment area who had done so many
times was already a pupil at White Lodge training with the Royal Ballet
since he was ten years old. So Philip Mosley was not involved at that time,
but did become a part of mining history in one sense as the person originally

113

interviewed at The Royal Opera House by the creators of *Billy Elliot*. But here the similarities end. Now Artistic Coordinator for The Royal Ballet at Covent Garden, his sense of loyalty to the community he was born in has never been in doubt.

Part two of the performance began with readings from the Grimethorpe Book.

The old Civic Hall in Barnsley had in its day hosted some of the biggest names with events from musical hall, theatre, lectures, politics and wrestling throughout its history, but I reckon those two nights could have ranked amongst the best of them. In the heart of the community spirit and increasingly worldwide support there was a euphoria which temporarily replaced the fear of what was to come. The play had never failed to reach its mark and with the additional power of the recorded words of the community those nights were equally powerful, with emotional ranks of scattered VIPs amongst local families and supporters.

When Tom Smith, the school's Head of Music, rounded off the first night of the two performances conducting what had become the hymn of the cause, *Jerusalem*, emotions were running high leaving many too overcome by emotion to join in. On the second night he rallied them with a rousing trumpet led rendition which had the entire assembly on its feet fortissimo. Even outside the hall in the corridors and out onto Eldon Street itself, proud parents and granddads in parked cars waiting to collect the children, or friends and even passers-by joined the chorus and so became a part of it.

As the audience left the theatre the response was equally positive. To ensure I would remember them for the school's next assembly, I made a note of the words of one man who waited to introduce himself and to say, 'I was proud to be here tonight; that was exactly what theatre is about and that production should be on in every school and theatre in this country.' I shook his hand, thanked him and asked his name. Only when I read the following review in the *Barnsley Chronicle* did I realise I had been talking to someone who, for more than one reason, knew what he was talking about.

John Kelly was not only the inspiration and driving force behind the creation of Barnsley's own Lamproom Theatre; he was also another ex-miner who had worked at Grimethorpe pit and the man whose review of the performance appeared in the newspapers including the *Barnsley Chronicle*.

Pupils put on unique mining show.

WHEN the President of the Board of Trade announced on October 13 1992 that 31 collieries, including Grimethorpe, were to be closed, the response from Willowgarth High School and the local community was instantaneous.

With assistance from Glass Houghton-based publishers Yorkshire Arts Circus, the pupils, staff and local volunteers compiled a volume of comments and reminiscences about the closure of their pit and created a wonderful little book entitled 'Energy for Coal'.

Last week a talented troupe from Willowgarth High School brought the book and their performing skills to the Civic Theatre and presented two thought-provoking performances of words and music entitled 'An Evening of Mining History'.

The first part of the presentation concerned itself with the historical text of the inquiry into the Huskar Pit disaster of 1839 when 26 children between the ages of seven and 17 were drowned when a torrential flash flood swept into a drift gate.

The account of this apalling incident - called 'Children of the Dark' - was compiled by Jack Brown, Cliff Laycock and Donald McKelvie and it recalled the bleak conditions that our recent forefathers endured to satisfy the nation's thirst for coal-fired energy.

The second half of the production comprised readings from the Grimethorpe book and illustrated the shock and frustration of a community who after 98 years of dedication to coal production, now find themselves accused of being surplus to requirement.

The pupils and staff of Willowgarth High School were ably assisted throughout by the talented 'No Man's Band and Betty Martin', who linked the spoken recitals with traditional folk songs and new music by local writers. They also included Alex Glasgow's rather apt song — 'Close The Coalhouse Door'.

Despite the obvious intensity of the subject matter, it has to be said that the production - through its brilliant conception and presentation - was absorbing and ironic.

It must surely rate among the very best of this season's theatrical events.

Directed by Cheryl McCanaan and produced by Mel Dyke with technical direction and staging by Dick Walker and Mark Britton respectively, a most memorable evening of theatre and mining history included the following performers -

Victoria Boyden, Gary Clarke, Katie Dalton, Mark Fairweather, Nicholas Handley, Martin Homer, Caroline Lister, Katrina Marriott, Dayle Moore, Christopher Peach, Deborah Tate, Donna Ward, Dave Ardron, Roger Beswick, Bob Bone, Janet Dalton, Chris Davison, Graham Bradbury, Rebecca Cooper, Marie Day, Scott Haigh, Rebecca Hanson, Tracey Hutchinson, Stacey Lodge, Joanne Mason, Kerry Neale, Ben Saxton, Claire Upton, Donna White, Mel Dyke, Margaret Ferry, Cheryl McCanaan, Tom Smith, Ron Wilby, Oliver Brooke, Richard Cooper, Carrie Dent, Matthew Hancock, Joanne Hardy, Sarah King, Michelle Lunn, David Meggitt, Joy Nicholas, Darren Smith, Julia Utley.

By kind permission of the *Barnsley Chronicle*

Willowgarth High School and Grimethorpe's contribution to highlight the sheer folly and worse, of the pit closures through the number and range of activities which were undertaken gained international recognition. It should be noted however that throughout the campaign the community's thoughts were with and shared by thirty other communities in similar states of concern, anxiety and fear.

These were the other thirty pits also initially threatened with closure:

Easington	Vane Tempest	Westoe
Prince of Wales	Sharlston	Maltby
Frickley	Markham Main	Bentley
Rossington	Hatfield	Houghton Main
Kiveton	Levercotes	Bilsthorpe
Calverton	Clipstone	Cotgrave
Rufford	Silverhill	Bolsover
Markham	Shirebrook	Silverdale
Betwy	Taff Merthyr	Trentham
Parkside	Point of Air	Wearmouth

Chapter 8

Downing Street

Women against Pit Closures were at the outset mostly relatives of miners, but quickly became a wide-ranging inclusive national and international group of women. Many with no connections to the industry, aware of the disastrous impact of the steel closures in nearby Sheffield, were now supportive during that period of the official NUM struggle to keep pits open and communities alive.

Inevitably they set up a camp outside Grimethorpe Colliery and it, and visitors to it, became a part of everyday life in the village. My recollection is that it was a friendly and informative base with an unthreatening atmosphere, a commune with a purpose made up largely of the mothers and aunts of the children we were teaching. Well known faces of politicians, actors, musicians, journalists and a big favourite Sue Johnson visited it, as did I and other staff on many occasions to sit and chat over a cup of coffee. Ann Scargill and Betty Cook visited the school and explained their role in the campaign. And it was from the WAPC headquarters that the offer came to ask me if they could help take the Grimethorpe book to Downing Street. To present a copy of the book to the then Minister Prime John Major, and to highlight that it was a whole community issue, the children voted for who should go, and two girls who ironically were not miners' daughters went with me. Claire Geeson was twelve years old at the time and Sally Middleton was fifteen, and their selection was really a clear indication of how united the community was. They were voted for by the pupils as having evidenced ability to express their concerns about the impending closures rationally and articulately.

The girls turned out to be an even better choice than the random selection could have promised. We were met at the train by Annie Marjoram representing WAPC who took us by taxi to Downing Street. On the way she explained that, with our approval, three other women in support of the book would join us there which would be even more likely to engage media coverage of the event. On arrival we saw how that could well be as a smiling Alison Steadman and Shadow Minister for Education Ann Taylor joined us with a message from Helena Kennedy apologising profusely that she would have to miss coming to help as she had unexpectedly been called to attend High Court.

On arrival at No 10, the door was opened by a stern-faced gentleman in a black suit. Sally smiled and explained that the school had been part of a community project to record the life of one of the pits due to be closed and handed him the book. She glanced at me when he then asked where the letter was but Claire quickly replied it was not a letter, just the book, to which he patiently explained that there should be a covering letter to explain to the Prime Minister what the book was about. The twelve-year-old responded equally politely that it was a very short book so if the prime Minister just read it he would know what it was about!

That caused a fair bit of laughter and the girls were immediately called over to join the ranks of journalists and photographers opposite No 10. To me it was a massively intimidating sight and I am still overwhelmed by the confidence bordering on panache that those two schoolgirls exhibited in giving the first ever interviews in their lives, in the face of the world's media. To the girls it appeared to be less so at the time judging from the professionalism of their performances. The original reason for the book had been in part to give youngsters a chance to observe, analyse and comment on their own perspective of the community in which they were living. They certainly did that!

Nearly twenty years later I was interested to establish what, if any, of the experiences had affected their progress or remained with them. I went back to talk to Claire Geeson who had left Willowgarth School at sixteen and completed her A level in Law at night school whilst working full time for a firm of Barnsley solicitors. Subsequently working her way up to become PA to a Partner in the firm Claire Garrity was now working as an Associate of the Chartered Institute of Legal Executives in a Wakefield firm, a married woman and mother of two children Olivia and Finlay when I went to meet her again in 2011.

I asked her what had stood out most for her that day and it was a fascinating and motley list that she reeled off. The instant response was the bit which initially scared her, the sight of the 'furry sound microphone' moving in towards her face as she was bombarded with questions in an interview which her family and friends would have already proudly seen on national television before she got back home that evening. The rest flooded back in sporadic disorganised memories and ranged from the trivial to the momentous:

'I thought it was absolutely great, I felt really grown up choosing magazines to read on the train!

I recognised Alison Steadman from TV straight away and wondered, why is this famous person doing all this in her own time, just to meet two schoolgirls?

The noise and flashing of cameras outside No 10 was deafening.

Alison Steadman's involvement in the visit to Downing Street was a highlight of the day. Photograph by kind permission of Alison Steadman

I had no idea we would be searched at Security on arrival at the Houses of Parliament.

I was stunned seeing Margaret Thatcher quite a presence in a moss grey suit standing a few feet away looking just like her spitting image model, an authority figure giving off 'no messing' signals.

Going into the Lobby of the House of Commons – I had never having seen so many men in suits before, realising then how few women there were.

Being allowed onto the Terrace to be photographed with MPs and seeing the River Thames from a completely different view.

I didn't think we would be introduced to MPs and journalists in the Green Room in Parliament; that was really something else!'

I wondered if there were any disappointments on the day.

'Tuna salad! I didn't like to say at the time but I never liked tuna. I only ordered it because I couldn't see another vegetarian option and didn't know if I could ask for one.'

Interestingly, she added that if she had understood then the full implications of what was entailed, she probably wouldn't have gone but she was so glad she didn't know, as at the end of the day and to this day she had no regrets whatsoever. She also reckons the experience contributed greatly to her confidence and led to her wanting to be a part of a major International Women's Day at the school two years later.

Chapter 9

Balloons

Houghton Main Women Against Pit Closures had organised a hot air balloon to set off from their camp outside the pit in the hope that it would travel from there to Grimethorpe and Barnsley and with a good wind, on to Doncaster and Markham Main flying a banner saying 'Not 31, not 21, not 10 not 1: no pit closures!'

Back at Willowgarth, the Science, Maths and Geography departments were quick off the mark in spotting the potential to maximise the enthusiasm raised by the idea's practical opportunities to address the National Curriculum, though I have to confess I did not at that stage foresee it as potential for any unique or lasting inspiration in the Arts. The Science department took up every possible element to maintain interest, with a popular experiment to find how far from Grimethorpe the properties of helium could take a small balloon. Virtually every child wanted to be involved, requiring almost a thousand balloons and the helium. Instantly supportive the Coal Communities Campaign Chairman Hedley Salt contacted the Campaign officers who readily organised the balloons and the helium. Each balloon complete with the sender's name, was released over a three-day period.

We were increasingly aware by this time of how much support nationwide there was to keep the pits open, so were optimistic in expecting returns. There was to be a prize for the person whose balloon travelled furthest, so many children added a brief personal message on the tags, which also had the school's name and 'Help us save OUR PIT'.

By the middle of the following week by word of mouth, telephone calls and many written replies came flooding in, from all manner of individuals and groups, some addressed to the whole school – others as personal messages to the individual child. The first tag to be returned was from Leamington Primary School followed by a wide selection:

Reg.	Period 1		Period 2		Period 3		Reg.	Period 4		Period 5	
	ST SUB	ROOM	ST SUB	ROOM	ST SUB	ROOM		ST SUB	ROOM	ST SUB	ROOM
	55 9H4 F*	A36	31 7WH/L PE		38 10 M*	A112		27 8WG H*	B108	21 11 S1	C10
	23 9H3 F*	A39	15 7WH/L PE		10 10 M*	A114		48 8WT PH	B11	30 11 S1	C102
	20 9H1 F*	AN3	32 7HC E*	AN4	47 10 M*	A115		14 8WB PH	B15	08 11 S1	C105
	29 9H2 F*	AN4	13 7HC E Sup.	AN4	11 10 M*	A116		30 8HL S*	C105	39 11 S1	C108
	39 9W4 S	C108	49 7WE G*	B103	44 10 M*	A119		43 8HS E*	C27	03 11 S1	C109
	03 9W1 S	C109	50 7HH H	B106	40 10 M*	A35		01 8HP E**	C30	33 11 S1	C5
	33 9W3 S	C5	46 7HB G*	B3	52 10 M*	B5		24 8HP E Sup.	C30	06 11 S1	C8
	06 9W2 S	C8	36 7WS RE*	B9	21 10 M*	C10		57 8WH S*	CN101	37 11 S1	CN112
			22 7HA E	C11				37 8HF RE	CN112		

N.B. STAFF AND PUPILS MUST REPORT TO THEIR USUAL ROOMS. AN ESCORT WILL ARRIVE AT SOME POINT DURING THE LESSON AND ACCOMPANY EACH GROUP IN ITS TURN TO THE DESIGNATED AREA.

The balloon project was carefully organized to involve all children without disruption to other lessons.

Mr T R Robson – Calverton Notts 'Muck-spreading land near Calverton – a pit also under – threat found 2 balloons, 1 at 1 30, 1 at 5 30 on March 3 1993.'

Mr and Mrs Hallam, Skegby Sutton-in-Ashfield – their children Kathleen 14 Robert 12 wanted to know how their school could become involved.

The Earl of Lanesborough, – simply 'Thinking of you!'

Roy Smith – Bulwell Hill Park; an ex-miner wrote 'Good luck to you my girl.'

Shelthorpe School Loughborough – 'We're with you.'

W Hopkin, Watnall Weather Centre – 'Found by a man from DH Lawrence's home town Eastwood.'

Graham Wilcock – 'Ex-miner 31 years at Shirebrook Colliery – I'm proud of you.'

Hollingwell Golf Course Notts – 'Best wishes from all four of us!'

Paddy Hanrahan – Pleasley Wood 'I'm a retired miner Shirebrook.'

Mr W L Harvey – '38 and a half years Shirebrook, now redundant.'

C D Allett – 'I'm an ex-miner from Wolvey, Leics – Keep it up!'

Aston Comprehensive – 'With all our good wishes.'

Farmer Brian Roketh – Hill Farm Tollerton Notts 'found it whilst out driving my tractor!'

Valley Farm – Barnards Castle County Durham.

Derek Roberts – Warren Wood Ross-on-Wye. 'Best of luck against Tory Destroyers.'

Mr D Impey – Alverchurch Birmingham – 'Found it in the swimming pool.'

Jeanette and Diane – Arnold Notts 'Write back please and tell us how the campaign goes.'

Mrs Walters – Thieves Wood, Kirkby-in-Ashfield – 'I marched in Hyde Park!'

Hints Village between Lichfield and Tamworth – 'Keep going!'

East Midlands Airport – 'From everyone here – GO FOR IT!'

Association of University Teachers, University of Nottingham – 'How can we help?'

Mrs D Brown – Natwest Bank, Shepshed 'Congratulations!'

Lisa Coates – Repton High School 'We support your efforts.'

Ian Mather – Shirebrook ex-miner 'Told everybody on my mobile phone…'

G M Page – North Mansfield – enclosed £10 for the Community Fund.

Megan Thomas – Wollaton Notts.

'My Daddy works at Ollerton and my Uncle Robin at Cotgrave – thank you.' £10 for *Save our Pits*.

Peter Miller – Director ANSEC Ltd Mining Consultants.

J G Cole – 28 Lea Hall Lane Brereton Rugeley 'You are great kids!'

Wayne and Cheryl Fisher – Arnold Notts 'just visited Wombwell for the first time a week ago for our family history!'

Dr S H Harrison on his rounds in Mansfield – 'Save All Our Pits!'

Mrs Bradshaw West Bridgeford – 'LOVE YOUR BAND!'

Class 4 – Melbury Primary School Nottingham found it out on a field study – 'We're fighting with you!'

Branston Family – Syston Leics 'Best wishes – we use coal on our fire!'

Wootton of Woodstock – 'Best wishes.'

There was a good wind on the first day, and a change of direction twice overnight sending the balloons in all four different directions. Interestingly the returns indicate a full range of support from professionals to redundant miners, and from all age groups. I did hope the return from the Earl of Lanesborough was actually from the 9th Duke and not from the regulars of a pub in Kegworth, and happily it was. However, Baroness Wootton was not she of Woodstock who had sadly had died in 1988, so I suspect the last entry was from the villagers or the local school in Wootton-by-Woodstock. My own personal commiserations are still with the child whose balloon stuck on the school fence so never even left the grounds. But no-one would have wagered that one would travel as far as the south coast – and then made it over the Channel? Found in Brittany and returned to the school with a note on the tag which was still intact:

From FRANCOIS GRALL
'Bon Chance! I found this whilst working in my artichoke field in Kernevez Cleder near Saint Pol-de-Leon, Brittany.'

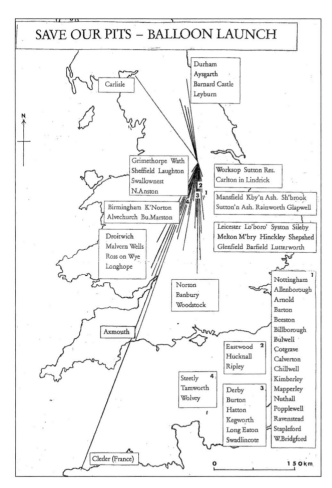

SAVE OUR PITS – BALLOON LAUNCH

Durham
Aysgarth
Barnard Castle
Leyburn

Carlisle

N

Grimethorpe Wath
Sheffield Laughton
Swallownest
N.Anston

Worksop Sutton Res.
Carlton in Lindrick

Birmingham K'Norton
Alvechurch Bu.Marston

Mansfield Kby'n Ash. Sh'brook
Sutton'n Ash. Rainworth Glapwell

Droitwich
Malvern Wells
Ross on Wye
Longhope

Leicester Lo'boro' Syston Sileby
Melton M'bry Hinckley Shepshed
Glenfield Barfield Lutterworth

Norton
Banbury
Woodstock

Nottingham
Allenborough
Arnold
Barton
Beeston
Billborough
Bulwell
Cotgrave
Calverton
Chillwell
Kimberley
Mapperley
Nuthall
Popplewell
Ravenstead
Stapleford
W.Bridgford

Axmouth

Eastwood
Hucknall
Ripley

Steetly
Tamworth
Wolvey

Derby
Burton
Hatton
Kegworth
Long Eaton
Swadlincote

Cleder (France)

0   150km

Arrival points logged for where balloons were found – North, East, West and further South than any believed possible.

To the north they reached Cumbria's west coast, over to the east coast of County Durham. What remains most significant was the density of returns from the coal-rich and industrial spine of the country, spread by a predominantly north easterly wind through the Northumberland, Yorkshire, Derbyshire, Notts and Leicestershire coalfields. The map was what really pinpointed geographic and demographic areas of interest, or comparatively a lack of it in number but also whether they contained a message which reflected understanding of the situation. Was it direction or the strength of the wind that seemed to have blown it over the heads of people in leafy coal-less suburbs or the south of the country? Was it a lack of empathy, an unawareness of the implications of this particular policy, or a just lesson that would not have meaning for people who lived in those areas until twenty years later?

Gary Clarke was twelve years old when he released his balloon. It didn't go very far he tells me so he wasn't a winner in that league table on that day.

Influenced by Willowgarth Head of Drama Cheryl McCanaan's teaching skills, he first played a child miner victim of an 1838 mining tragedy for the school's 1993 production of *Children of the Dark*.

Early stage indications of political awareness, shown here, third child from the left, at the visit of former Leader of the Labour Party, Neal Kinnock's visit to the school.

Neil Kinnock's visit to the school shows a young Gary Clark, 3rd from left. Photograph Willowgarth High School collection

Balloons

In 1998, as the first recipient of the Brian Glover Award for Outstanding Achievement in Performing Arts, Gary Clarke graduated from The Electric Theatre Studios at Barnsley Sixth Form College, where Principal Jenny Miccoli recalls, 'Gary's energy and emotion were beyond imagination; he was inspirational to teach.'

His tutor Liz McPolin clearly identifies him as unique:

'From humble beginnings at a time of educational and economic decay, Gary has risen almost phoenix-like from the ashes and turmoil of a neglected but never broken community. Gary's journey stands like a beacon for those who follow in his footsteps who dare "take a chance" and break the mould of the narrow aspirations often imposed by state education. The journey is testament to his home, to his talent and above all to his tireless willingness to work and take risks. The scrawny boy, who I encountered in 1996, had boundless energy and a naivety which gave me a blank canvas upon which to build the first foundations in giving him a grasp of choreographic principles and unlocking his inner creativity. Highly receptive, he absorbed new concepts and knowledge, trusted my guidance and broke the monotony of rehearsal with his legendary impersonations. He finished his time at Barnsley College with his momentous performance of *Death and the Maiden* in 1997.

He remains a close friend, an inspirational role model for the young people of Barnsley and beyond. His frequent return visits as a professional artist or simply sharing a coffee remains a huge pleasure in my life. As he moves from performer/choreographer to the totally defined choreographer, I believe his work will now evolve at pace and direction. Above all, I pray he will continue to articulate through movement the life expectations, fears and aspirations of a part of the world and a segment of society too readily discarded by our political masters.

Gary has been an inspiration but above all he is a dear friend.'

Graduation next from the Northern School of Contempory Dance in 2001 came with a reputation of equally high regard:

'Gary is such an exciting artist because his work is deeply rooted in personal experience whilst always speaking to an audience. His humour, physicality, vision and sheer imagination are utterly captivating. He is inspirational to young people and to the non-dance specialists he works with on a range of community projects. His dedication to using every possible resource to put on a show is infectious and young people love working with him because he is challenging them to be the best they can be: whether in a straightforward dance piece, a flash mob or a bonkers murder mystery party performance.'

So says Wieke Eringa the Artistic Director of Yorkshire Dance who has known and worked with him since then. That will doubtless be why he is still an Associate Artist there and has been a Yorkshire Dance Patron since 2004, which alongside other ongoing recognition and ever expanding lists of awards, evidence his seriously impressive achievements.

There are few who are capable of combining the artistic qualities of Gilbert and George with the unique comedy of Morecambe and Wise to create what he calls 'foolish shenanigans and nonsense' and from 2006 on have it playing from Bulgaria to Barnsley and The Royal Opera House to Sheffield's Crucible. Bringing the innovative back home can be tough in any field, but he produced it on his home turf at the Lamproom Theatre in 2011 and brought a full house to its feet.

His 2007 production of *COAL* was created through his own memories of the closure years intended to be more a physical exploration than a balletic critique. The impact of that 1992 government policy for him, as for many others, left a legacy of pain which is still raw in 2012. What really marks him out as outstanding though is that he evidences the ability to rise above such imposed demoralisation. He has the true mark of a creative artist, to choose not to be defeated by any experience. I haven't discussed literature or language with him since he was child, but I am willing to gamble that he shares my take of Oscar Wilde's view:

> *To regret one's own experiences is to arrest*
> *one's own development.*
> *To deny one's own experiences is to put a lie*
> *on the lips of one's own life.*

Nearly twenty years on, in 2012, the award winning choreographer is back in Barnsley en route to the Edinburgh Festival with his semi-autobiographical newest work *A Beautiful Hell.*

High achiever Gary Clark, but with feet in pit boots and still firmly on the ground.
Photograph by kind permission of Gary Clark

Asking if I also remember the balloons he tells me:

'My work is a vehicle to convey episodes of my own life with mining history which are both nostalgic and brutal. Horsemeat and COAL expose feelings of a sense of alienation, and the tension of the shattering of my childhood that is with me still. Thatcher destroyed my village, leaving me with a need to represent the history of that era through physicality.'

His dark metaphor of shattered black lungs equates and contrasts with the bursting of balloons. The memory of the London bound Scottish miners' feet on the ground with hopes flying high match his own aspiration and strength of purpose. But it is the energy-fuelled day they released the balloons which resonates in his mind and re-surfaces in his work as powerfully as any other inspiration. I wonder if sees the same irony that I do when I learn that one educational course in which he involved is – Aim Higher!

'In 2012, the Jubilee year, I was invited to a reception at Buckingham Palace to meet The Queen and the Duke of Edinburgh and was amongst people like Dame Helen Mirren, Kevin Spacey and Michael McIntyre to name but a few. It felt like one of the biggest achievements of my life, and at the time and I remember thinking, how has a lad from Grimethorpe got here? It was an amazing moment and brought home to me just how your education can impact on your life.'

Recognition at international levels of his choreography, performing skills, writing, and teaching at universities around the globe, plus involvement with virtually every major dance company world wide, confirm that he himself is now by any definition, a very high flier. So though his feet are symbolically still in pit boots; there is no doubt that Gary Clarke has earned and won his place in that premier league table today:

'If you squeezed Gary Clarke into a time capsule, buried it and brought it out in years to come, a heady reminder of the politically turbulent and poptastic 80's and 90's would leap out like a crazed jack-in-a-box. Not just a social one but the zeitgeist of those decades, in contemporary dance too.' 'Londonist'.'

Chapter 10

Everyman, Closure and Sheffield Coal Week

Then just as soon as 'The Review' allowed in the first week in May 1993, the balloon burst and the deepest mine in the UK was gone. The Headmaster wrote to the local branch of the NUM:

Mr Ken Hancock
NUM Grimethorpe Branch
12 May 1993

Dear Ken

Just a note to confirm my continued support and sympathy. I know that I can speak for my colleagues here at school in saying that we were gutted to hear of the pit's closure. The Government's and British Coal's tactics have been a constant source of amazement and sorrow to me during the past months.

I have nought but sympathy for those miners pressured by management to accept redundancy. Were I in their position I doubt whether I have would have had the personal courage they have shown for so long. Everyone must consider the best interests of his family, and the pressure has been intolerable. In my view – for what is worth – NUM members at Grimethorpe have earned the right to hold their heads high in any company, anywhere. They have always had my respect and admiration and all that has happened in the present bad times has only served to increase that respect. I wish them and their families every good fortune in rebuilding their lives.

I am glad that our common cause has brought the school closer to its community, though I wish we had deepened that rapport under better circumstances. Please be assured that we shall continue to support you and your members in any way we can.

Yours sincerely

A J Dorney
Headteacher. (Copied to me by the Head for information to all staff)

It had not been an unhappy campaign, far from it. The community and far beyond was unified and all the feedback was that the school's activities were thought to have been inspiring or fun to do and worth the effort for that, and for the learning curves. The march through London had brought back stories of cheers from office windows in the West End and thumbs up from posh ladies in two-piece tweed suits on Kensington High Street, with wry comments of changing times. According to one miner who had been there, 'Eight years earlier the reputation of miners had been the scum of the earth if you believed the tabloids.' With hindsight the public might choose to reflect more carefully in whose interests that may have been. 'That day, though, everybody loved us.'

Richard Alwyn's 1990s BBC TV *Everyman* film had observed first hand the impact of the closures. In 2012, I spoke to him again for the first time since then, telling him I had just obtained an updated copy of it and asked if he remembered the programme amongst so many others. His immediate response was to ask if he could still be heard filming in the background at the launch of a book in a day, as Gail Hancock read her poem aloud, he was so overcome that he sobbed.

The program also evoked an unusually high response from the south of the country, this one from Buckingham.

Then on 7 May 1993, despite such support world wide, its fate already sealed in 1992 if not before, Grimethorpe pit was bricked up and shut down. Not forgotten however, continuing use of music, stories, films, theatre poetry, dance and recorded memories of that moment in time will remain.

Award-winning radio presenter Simon Hirst is best known for his wit, rants and banter on *Hirsty's Daily Dose*, or as an incredibly popular DJ. But he has a serious side too:

'My Dad wasn't a miner, but his brother Albert was along with my Grandad & Uncle Geoff on my Mum's side of the family. My

Everyman, Closure and Sheffield Coal Week

Grandad Coates worked on the coalface at Ferrymoor until an accident forced him to become a Steel Bobby at Houghton Main. Unfortunately I never got to talk to him about his time down the pit, as he sadly passed away in January 1973 aged just forty-eight.

What I do remember about the coal industry and our family was my Uncle Geoffrey who worked at Grimethorpe pit from the age of

Dear Sir,

I watched "Everyman" last night and was so proud of all the miners + families who spoke.

I was also sickened at the trajic, short-sighted attitudes of people in Ivory Towers in London who have sold the birthright of our country and of yourselves + your children.

I have never written a letter before to either complain or compliment, and am writing this the morning after and not while anger still strong at the time of the programme

You have my support and I share your desperate anger. I am not clever with words but felt if I just bothered to write you might understand that there are a lot of people like me who support you, but feel helpless.

I hope your community survives, and seeing the good, quality, honest men you are - I really hope you do.

Merry Christmas to you all, I hope you get this letter.

seventeen through to taking one of the redundancy packages in 1990 when he was forty-eight. As he was single during the 1980s and lived in Cudworth, my parents would drop me off at his flat in Crown Avenue so he could look after me, whilst my mum and dad would spend their Saturday evening socialising. He would talk to me about his job, and I have vivid memories of him coming home straight from the pit without having showered once or twice. Seeing how dirty he was compared to how my dad looked after a hard day fixing and installing televisions, made me realise at an early age that this wasn't an easy or clean job made me even more interested about the history of our coal mining industry.

I grew up on council estate in Barnsley called Athersley North and our house was based at the top of the estate, which from my back bedroom gave a very good view of the skyline of Grimethorpe pit in the distance. I recall vividly standing at that window when I was eighteen and watching with a lump in my throat as the pit chimneys disappeared. Even though I'd never been down the pit in my life and hadn't tasted the same air as those brave miners did daily, I still felt real sad emotion that part of our history and industry was dying in front of my very eyes.

Working in radio for the majority of my life has given my access to meet some wonderful people. I was given the opportunity to interview Ewan McGregor on set of *Brassed Off*. We sat in a production unit and chatted about the plot of the film. As I listened to him talk with passion about the people of Grimethorpe who he had met during the months of filming, I was taken aback by how this was not just another actor playing a part in a film, but someone who had spent some time with the people of the village and understood the pain and turmoil they went through during the closure of their pit.

After the interview, I couldn't wait to see the film. I went to see it on the week of release at Barnsley Odeon, and after it finished drove straight to Grimethorpe to still see the signage 'In Cod We Trust' above the chip shop and then parked up where Pete Postlethwaite's character Danny collapses and looked towards the empty fields where the pit once stood. Again, I had a lump in my throat. I watched *Brassed Off* recently, and it's still a hugely powerful film, one that on release became an instant classic. It reflected the end of an era but the beginning of awareness in me of

The Revd. Canon JANE SINCLAIR MA

The Cathedral Church of SS. Peter & Paul · Sheffield

THE CATHEDRAL SHEFFIELD S1 1HA
Telephone 0742 753434 · Fax 0742 780244

JEMS/JAF

24 June 1993

Mrs Mel Dyke
Willowgarth High School
Brierley Road
GRIMETHORPE
S72 7AJ

Dear Mrs Dyke

I would like to write to thank you and your colleagues very much indeed for your contributions to the service celebrating Coal held in Sheffield Cathedral last Sunday. Various people from the church and well beyond the church have told me how moved they were by your readings. They certainly brought the reality of life in the Mining Industry at the moment home to the congregation. Thank you for the time and trouble which you took to prepare your readings.

With all good wishes for the remainder of your term.

Yours sincerely

Canon Jane Sinclair

These responses reflect the range of hitherto silent support.

the cynicism in big business, like the Tara Fitzgerald character whose job was a lie, just to cover up the already decided closure.

I am guessing that most pits were alike, but it was the band that made this pit different. I heard them play a couple of years ago at Emmanuel Church in Barnsley. I was front row, and the vibrations thrilling through the audience's bodies and mine was electric.

I wish I had been at that Westminster Abbey service.

I'm fascinated by our town's history and buildings that we have. I recently pulled up outside the NUM Headquarters' at the top of Old Mill Lane, and just stood and looked at Graham Ibbeson's family statue outside. I think the majority of people drive and walk past it daily. But next time you are passing, stop and spend sometime looking to understand the power and meaning of it along with remembering those who lost their lives in times of struggle.

The audience who listen to my radio shows are predominantly young, although we do have our older listener. The majority though will have never come into contact with someone who worked down the pit, or held a piece of coal. It's all in their past family history that hopefully one day they will research just like I am.

I mentioned earlier that my dad didn't work down the pit, so we immediately as a family unit in Athersely were not affected by the strike, but I recall the utter unified hatred for Thatcher as child in 1984. I can clear as day remember a water problem at my junior school St Hilda's, and not being able to use the toilets' or wash our hands, and who's fault was it in the mind of nine-year-olds. Thatcher's!

The memories of walking over the field from Cudworth towards the Coalite plant with my Uncle Chris, as we went me meet my Uncle Geoff after he finished work will stay with me forever. I can still feel the freezing cold dark air, the flickering lights of Grimethorpe pit in the distance, along with THAT smell.

I'll never forget it for as long as I live. A priceless memory...'

There was a change of mood a sense of loss, anger, a massive anti climax and worry. Then we were invited to take part in Coal Week to be held in a packed Sheffield Cathedral the following month. *Children of the Dark* again, with readings from the book: and no less than the Archbishop of Canterbury George Carey. His words stay with me still:

'that these days would be remembered as the time when the Church stood so firmly in support of the working class, and not the establishment.'

Chapter 11

International Women's Day

In 1995 the continuing ramifications of the closures were still proving to create adverse effects on students in terms of motivation and opportunities. Traditionally, girls who had married well qualified electrical or mechanical engineers, or the high earning strong young face workers had been well placed in the community ranking. It was thought not only acceptable to be 'just a housewife' in those circumstances, but desirable. I remember well one parent on completing the entry form for her child's admission to the school reminding us not too sharply, that she had 'the best job in the world' as she wrote 'I'm a full time wife and mother.'

Arguably some girls were distracted from maximising their own educational and career prospects and ironically it was the loss of mining careers for men which brought a knock-on effect for women. In some cases it allowed women who had actually under-achieved to take the opportunity to seek further educational or career development. Others were forced into a new world of work with varying experiences and outcomes. For far too many families one aspect hit hard; the despairing lack of purpose, a contagious disability which comes with the sense of worthlessness and hopelessness imposed by imposed mass unemployment. It stultifies interest, effort ambition, aspiration, motivation, and even hope. The only antidote was shared community spirit. It had lain dormant for a year or so, but now flourished again.

In my last year at Willowgarth a unique opportunity to highlight the impact felt by the pit closures in terms of youth unemployment came up. The school was approached by the Youth Information Service offering the chance for a team of women staff and girls to be trained to abseil down a high building and take part in an exercise to raise awareness of an impending International Women's Day. It soon became clear as we discussed it that it presented a far wider range of opportunities, and even a total re-think of the needs of the entire community. Deputy Head Roger

Beswick suggested and took on the mammoth task of re-writing the entire timetable for one day in response to my suggestion of a whole school role reversal day. It caused an initial stir, but gained the immediate support of the Head, Senior Management, Governors and eventually it seemed the whole school. The regular timetable was abandoned and in its place a series of activities in which boys and male members of staff mainly carried out tasks which stereotypically would normally have been done by girls, and vice versa. Sessions were run by sixty or so expert visitors for a programme of classes ranging from Aerobics and Anorexia to Xenophobia and Zen Buddhism and nearly everything in between. Claire Geeson was one of the abseil team which she remembers being organised by members of staff Bev Vosper, Cheryl McCanaan and Debbie Allen.

'I couldn't even climb the wall on the much smaller first practice run at Hoyle Mill, but I had committed to doing the big abseil and was determined to see it through. I was petrified really but was caught up with the excitement of it all, so I carried on and was ok at the next trial attempt in Derbyshire. Then it really was exciting – doing the big one on the day down the Cudworth viaduct. I'm still proud of having done it now!'

A great day for girls! By kind permission of Sheffield Newspapers

The Star, Wednesday, March 8, 1995 — LOCAL NEWS — 9

Live life to the full

Messages of support

ALL Willowgarth pupils were today involved in activities to raise awareness of women's issues. Deputy head Mel Dyke wrote to successful women to ask for their support.

"I was once asked: How can you tell when you finally become a woman? My reply was: 'When you compare your wage packet with that of a man doing the same job." - ACTRESS MAUREEN LIPMAN.

"The opportunities for women to participate in a modern society are enormous. Opening girls' eyes to these opportunities is always valuable." - VIRGINIA BOTTOMLEY.

"The sexes are always going to be different, thank God. social changes affect patterns of behaviour but we have to complement each other, not compete and fight." - ACTRESS EILEEN DERBYSHIRE.

Some of the Willowgarth High School pupils who were celebrating International Women's Day today with scores of events

International Women's Day

ACTIVITIES

01	Mrs A Bailey	70 years of Labour Party
02	Gennie Evans	Karaoke
03	Melanie Purkins	Improving the School Garden
04	Sharon Curran & Heather Marsh	Improving the School Environment – paths
05	Rita Poole & Gill Best	First Aid
06	N.A.C.R.O	Community Development
07	Avril Todd & Pat Howarth	Careers – Letters of Application
08	Karen Brunton	Team Building/Co-operation
09	Colin Watson	Catering
10	Sandra Barnes	Child Abuse
11	Linda Smith	Assertiveness
12	Rita Brown & Dawn Hancock	Health Advice
13	Dr Davis Reynolds	Health Advice
14	Vera Holling	Flower Arranging
15	Mo Bone	Women's Refuge
16	Berwin's	Practical Skill Test
17	Flt. Lft. Nikola Bill	Problem Solving
18	Dr Mary Jefferson	The Role of Women in Peru
19	Marie Bedford	The Role of Army Wives in Germany
20	Anne Phipps	Women's Lives in East Germany
21	Mike Miller	Women in Japan
22	Gaele Levy	The French Perspective
23	Janet Wood	Percussion Workshop
24	Fiona Patterson	Writer's Workshop
25	Sarah Walmsley	Women and Art in English
26	Sara Maitland	Writing Legends and Gender
27	Chrissie Yates	Racism and Equal Opportunities
28	Annette Woodward	Gender Issues
29	Maggie Loy	Media Images
30	Jane Holland	Dance for Boys
31	Bridgid Kane	Self Awareness
32	Sister Broadhead	Health Advice
33	Leslie Frances	Hair Demonstrations
34	Sandra Woolridge	Trident
35	Kate Dodd	Personal Effectiveness
36	Jane Bradshaw	Options Aerobics
37	Mike Hill	Work Simulation – Earning & Living

38	Derek Emms	Road Safety
39	Yvonne Preston	Jewellery Manufacture
40	Jayne Manley	Cookery Competition & Food Design
41	Joanna Ruse	Barnsley Chronicle Reporters' Comp.
42	Kathleen Craggs	Women in the Third World
43	Ray Ashton	Catering
44	Jackie Bone	Individual Needs – Celebrities' Letters
45	Army Assault	Army Assault Course
46	Martin Mathew	Music Workshop
47	Tom Smith	Music Workshop
48	Colin Jones	Votes for Women
49	R.A.F	Careers in the R.A.F
50	Army	Careers in the Army
51	Barnsley & Doncaster T.E.C	The Edge
52	Janet Pearson	Running Your Own Business

All departmental staff were involved in making cross curricular links to the day's events Staff Inputs: with additional support from area coordinators – Dr Dorney, Mel Dyke, Roger Beswick, Bev Vosper, Tracy Allot, Jenny Tickle, Anne Harnett, Cheryl McCanaan, Janet Dalton, Jo Wiles, Tony Parkinson.

We decided to recruit support from role models outside our established connections and geographical range. For the idea to have maximum effect it was clear that ideas and nominees had to come from the youngsters themselves. Full school assemblies were initially used as briefing sessions to ensure that everyone was aware of what was to happen, then quickly became a channel for a flood of nominations. It soon became apparent that television was a main source of both entertainment and admiration. The difference between the two became fairly clear as suggestions flowed in not only from girls, the older boys also wanted to flag up who it was that they genuinely admired – or rather fancied.

It had been my intention to display all the originals of the responses along every corridor, so that near to every classroom in the building there would be influential messages of support and encouragement which the students would see as they passed. Wiser counsel from younger members of staff and some of the more reliable sources of information amongst the lads prevailed however, leading to copies being taken of all incoming letters and photographs and used for the displays. Wise counsel indeed as increasingly gaps along the walls began to appear flagging up favourites

Nominations from boys were heavily directed towards Gladiators. By kind permission of ITV and the "Gladiators".

now conspicuous by their absence. That the Gladiators were clearly in that pin-up league was indicated by the frequency with which their pictures, especially Lightening and Jet, went missing and had to be replaced on a regular daily basis.

If pressed for a personal favourite though I think it would have to be the nomination this material that recognition of that particular role has stayed in the vast majority of minds to the present day confirming it as one of the three all time international TV commercial greats. from one boy who suggested that his own mum was a great role model – 'She's brilliant; she's got a job and now my Dad's gone she looks after us three all on her own – she's like that woman on Oxo.' It occurred to me at that moment how effective that particular commercial was, and probably 'that woman' was representing the kind of family he wanted to be in or maybe had been once. Already a *Dr Who* Time Lord, Helen Herriot in *All Creatures Great and Small* and with a CV which included *Z Cars, Billy Liar, The Professionals* and the *Sweeney* on television, with as good a match on stage

Lynda Bellingham.

and in films, Lynda Bellingham really needed no introduction. But remarkably it was that power of television advertising which really showed itself by the number of other nominations for her as the universally popular young wife and the mother that everyone wanted to have in those Oxo commercials which she played for sixteen years. I hope Oxo is still paying her for flash back subliminal impact as, equally remarkably, I found in researching Lynda Bellingham's reply to the standard letter I sent to all nominees. Just as effective and uplifting now, it fired numerous assemblies and classroom debates. Now after reading her 2010 autobiography *Lost and Found*, I see I had missed the crucial point written between those lines. The subtle, sound and heart-felt advice was clearly there, but in times when soul-bearing was rare, the hidden pain behind it which gave it reality was far less obvious. This time she says exactly what's in the tin and the book's cover says it all:

'Looking back, perhaps the single biggest problem was fear. Fear mostly of failure, fear of other people – but mostly fear of myself. It has taken sixty years to discover who I really am. It's never too late to find yourself; however lost you may be...'

Nearly twenty years later, in 2012, whilst playing a lead role as Trish Stewart in the touring version of the West End smash *Calendar Girls*, she was first to support this book for the same reason, to motivate girls and women:

'An inspiring story of heartache and determination on the long road to wisdom and maturity. It's about getting through the tough times with the strong spirit of a survivor.'

But she did it.

```
                          The Old Vic



                          10th Jan 1995



To the pupils of WILLOWGARTH HIGH SCHOOL from LYNDA BELLINGHAM.


I wish you every sucess with your activities for the International
Women's Day.In the last thirty years I have been lucky enough to
be part of a very strong women's  movement in these years.It is
always changing and growing and one of the most valuable things
I have learnt is that women can be such good friends.The image
of women as sniping,gossiping ,unable to get with each other
is so far from the truth.We are very honest in the main and need
each other so much.Society will always be slow to change.I am
lucky in my profession as there has always been equality of
sorts.Not always financially...but we are working on that.But
certainly there is an attitude to acting that makes us equal in
the sense we are all trying to work in a profession that is
about communication.Male of female we are together as a team
This is not always the case I know.You young women must continue
to stand up for yourselves when necessary.It is not necessary
 to be aggressive I don't think.Understanding goes a long way
to creating openings for making points and persuading others to
your way of thinking.Always be proud of Womanhood and enjoy
your lives.It is a long and difficult road for men and women.
Nothing comes easy.So enjoy the travelling and the discovering
and keep strong.
```

with all good wishes

Lynda Bellingham

141

And that is virtually the same message she sent nearly twenty years ago along with a gift of an Oxo cookery book to be given as a fund raising prize. Both came with genuine apologies that she was unable to attend in person. And that was independently borne out by the excellent reviews of Wendy Wesserstein's play *The Sister's Rosenstein* at the Old Vic in which she played Pfeni one of the three sisters. By coincidence playing the other two sisters, Gorgeous and Sara respectively, Maureen Lipman and Janet Suzman also sent messages in support of the Grimethorpe project.

Maureen Lipman's letter gave food for thought:

'Women have moved onwards and upwards in their places in society since the great days of the Women's Movement but we are still just a taken in many areas, particularly politics and Science and the stress involved in running a career, a home and a family has not become easier. The idea of a crèche in any major office is still, unlike the rest of Europe, just an idea.'

Inspiration from famous faces came immediately. By kind permission of Maureen Lipman

Asked to complete a questionnaire by a tabloid newspaper to the question, 'how can you tell when you finally become a woman?' Her tongue-in-cheek reply was: 'When you compare your wage packet with that of a man's doing the same job.'

Soaps, and specifically the northern 'soaps', *Coronation Street* and *Emmerdale,* were big favourites too though, interestingly, despite its viewing figures, not one character from *Eastenders* was suggested.

Coronation Street's Sue Nichols was actually on leave when my letter arrived, but on return she rang the school offering to visit at another time and sending last minute good wishes.

Claire King, then *Emmerdale*'s elegant Kim Tate, sent a prize of a t-shirt, which caused not a little debate when we decided to award it to the best dressed girl on the day!

By kind permission of Claire King

Barnsley resident Kathy Staff and her alter ego, Nora Batty.
By kind permission of John and Kathy Staff

Best wishes,
Kathy Staff

Good Luck with the Project,
Kathy Staff

Rita Britton became a part of all the activities shown here updating Dame Jennie Murray

Supportive in 1995 and again backing Arts in Action in 2008.
By kind permission of the BBC and Kate Adie

Valerie Singleton sent a letter of encouragement which somewhat disappointed a couple of the lads who saw it as a poor result not being the free *Blue Peter* badge they had hoped for.

Journalists galore gave support and most nationally impressive to the girls were Barnsley girls; Jane Sanderson producer of *Women's Hour* along with presenter Jenni Murray, and nationally Kate Adie.

Coronation Street's Emily Bishop/Eileen Derbyshire was another who took the trouble to write why she felt strongly, and took a strong common sense line.

Prompt questions as to which favourite politician or writer I should write to for support widened the frame. Children's authors were especially popular and one of those rated as the very best were amongst the first to respond.

Berlie Doherty twice winner of The Carnegie Medal in Literature also represented a route of different choices, with wide and varied progress through a range of professional experience from social worker, post grad student, teacher, script and screenplay writer to major author.

Her own background was in a school where every child's last day would end with a film show of the great *Great Expectations*. Home was where parents and grandparents wrote poetry, stories and kept diaries, and encouraged a small child's belief that she could and should enter her own first attempts for reading on radio or even for publication. She wrote of her delight in seeing a school using so many interesting way to foster enjoyment and encouragement in giving such importance to awareness of International Women's Day.

Popular politicians included Mo Mowlam whose educational input had before she entered Parliament been highly valued locally at Northern College.

Estelle Morris was a major contributor and with Michael Clapham's support it was her recognition of the school's contributions which led to me being nominated as a representative on David Blunkett's Shadow Education Working Party. An experience which left me in no residual doubt whatever of the north/south divide!

Then MP for Redcar, Mo Mowlam, was all too aware of the impact on girls' job losses in coalfield communities. By kind permission of Mo Mowlam

Jude Kelly was wittily dismissive of any and all attempts to suppress aspiration.

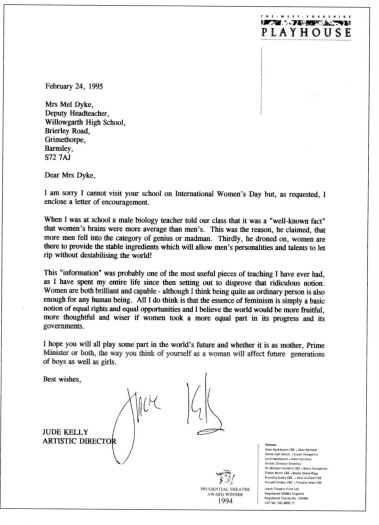

THE·WEST·YORKSHIRE
PLAYHOUSE

February 24, 1995

Mrs Mel Dyke,
Deputy Headteacher,
Willowgarth High School,
Brierley Road,
Grimethorpe,
Barnsley,
S72 7AJ

Dear Mrs Dyke,

I am sorry I cannot visit your school on International Women's Day but, as requested, I enclose a letter of encouragement.

When I was at school a male biology teacher told our class that it was a "well-known fact" that women's brains were more average than men's. This was the reason, he claimed, that more men fell into the category of genius or madman. Thirdly, he droned on, women are there to provide the stable ingredients which will allow men's personalities and talents to let rip without destabilising the world!

This "information" was probably one of the most useful pieces of teaching I have ever had, as I have spent my entire life since then setting out to disprove that ridiculous notion. Women are both brilliant and capable - although I think being quite an ordinary person is also enough for any human being. All I do think is that the essence of feminism is simply a basic notion of equal rights and equal opportunities and I believe the world would be more fruitful, more thoughtful and wiser if women took a more equal part in its progress and its governments.

I hope you will all play some part in the world's future and whether it is as mother, Prime Minister or both, the way you think of yourself as a woman will affect future generations of boys as well as girls.

Best wishes,

JUDE KELLY
ARTISTIC DIRECTOR

PRUDENTIAL THEATRE
AWARD WINNER
1994

Patrons
Alan Ayckbourn CBE • Alan Bennett
Dame Judi Dench • Susan Hampshire
Lord Harewood • John Harrison,
Artistic Director Emeritus
Sir Michael Hordern CBE • Barry Humphries
Trevor Nunn CBE • Dame Diana Rigg
Prunella Scales CBE • Paul Scofield CBE
Donald Sinden CBE • Timothy West CBE

Leeds Theatre Trust Ltd
Registered 926862 England
Registered Charity No. 255460
VAT No. 545 4890 17

Whilst the letters and photos were an undoubted eye catching success promoting interest and comparative discussions, the real meat of the day was in the range and quality of the activities on offer. I still meet ex pupils who remind me of that one off day in school and tell me it was one that they will always remember as fun and relevant information. I have no doubt that it was worth all the time, organisation and effort that staff, contributors, visitors and children put into it.

Sarah King's entry was short listed in the journalism competition and sums it up neatly:

'Women's Day is a major breakthrough in today's society. It isn't just about women but about males and females working together and having equal opportunities in the world. It's important to see that this Women's day is about all gender issues and is there to promote equal opportunities. In the past women's opinions haven't been valued, but we are all equal and all should have equal rights. This day gave us the chance of showing the achievements of past and present women to show the prospects for females in the surrounding area.

Willowgarth High School held an event on International Women's Day on Wednesday March 8th. It was a major success in showing a positive side to women and their attitudes. Men and females all took part in activities which were seen before as predominantly male or predominantly female. For example for the boys there was a chance to dance, with no women allowed in except the dance tutor. This was to promote the idea that dance isn't just a girls' subject and can be fun, as in the past dancing has been seen as a female only subject and the boys may have felt embarrassed especially in front of the girls. We found the boys were prepared to try harder when there were no females in the room, and so felt as if they had succeeded. This promoted an equal opportunity as the boys were being involved in something which had in the past been seen as 'cissy'.

Other activities included an Army assault course which was attended by both girls and boys, and as a result provided an opportunity to see that girls can be good as the boys as the Army is becoming a less and less male dominated work place. There was excitement and interest throughout the day and a positive look towards the future of Willowgarth and its pupils.

At last women's opinions and work are starting to be valued, and men and women can work together. A least the women of the past can know that their fight was the start of this new hope. Their voices live on in the women of today and will continue to do so until they have succeeded in making society equal in providing equal opportunities. There is no longer room for sexism in the 1990s.

As with everything, change takes time; but if we start early enough like this, perhaps old fashioned thoughts and ways will be forgotten and a new society created with us being equal in every possible way. Maybe now we will start to see a change.'

Chapter 12

Faith 2005

In the golden age of Hollywood, much of what I was taught by a fairly unreliable source, a twice weekly visit to see well and badly made films. As a small child I learnt the names and fates of Henry VIII's wives, not from History lessons but through film with Yorkshire born Charles Laughton's on screen dispatching of them. I didn't understand dramatic licence, bias or blatant slant. A proliferation of my father's favourite black and white Westerns clearly evidenced that the human race comprised only two easily identifiable types – goodies and baddies. All cowboys were goodies (with the odd exception of a bully who always rode a black horse), and all 'Indians' were baddies. That particular simplification bit the dust in 1950 with *Broken Arrow* bringing an early Technicolor admission that there may after all be a few good Indians. Twenty years on Dee Brown's 1970 Native American perspective publication *Bury My Heart at Wounded Knee* with rather more historical accuracy, retold the story of some good and some bad.

We call it perspective, intuition, instinct, philosophy or rationale, but what it seems to be at times is an innate sense of unsubstantiated conviction, a philosophy of 'don't try to confuse me with the facts when I've already made my mind up' or simple prejudice. West of the Kent coalfield and south of Leicester it was hard to find anyone who really understood either the reasons which led to the miners' strike of 1984–85, or the 'other side' of the case in the campaign against the 1992–93 pit closures. We had of course all read our chosen newspaper's version, or watched apparently undeniable televisual evidence of the sequence of events, only to learn in later years that evidence was not necessarily presented in the right order or sometimes may not have even been worth the money paid to obtain it.

The real Orgreave story is yet to be told at the time of writing.

Since then there have been plays, books, poems, films, musicals and even a ballet based on and around the rise and fall of the mining industry. I love that use of the Arts to transmit information, but have grown wary of fanciful artistic licence which masks factual inaccuracies, to create or re-write history. In 2010 I was invited to visit Los Angeles Valley College in Hollywood to speak to a group of sociology students in the Faculty of Labor History. It was at very short notice, a one-off which left no time for advanced reading to be set. The subject title I was given was 'Thatcher versus The Miners; A Grimethorpe Perspective.' So, true at least to my Hollywood infancy, I accepted the invitation on condition that in advance of the session, every student would have seen a film: either Mark Herman's astutely empathic *Brassed Off* or David Thacker's straight down the middle no holds barred 2005 BBC drama/documentary version *Faith*. They had! The outcome brought an unexpected response, with questions running over by two hours and an invitation to return annually. That was when it came home to me that the youth of America probably has no better understanding of our 'goodies or baddies' categorisation than I had of theirs in my childhood days. Nor did I realise that some stage or film heroes are for real, but I do now. Not only do we home grow them but if the loss of jobs here takes this young generation away they are homing pigeons Shaun Dooley, Kenny Doughty, Simon Hirst, Philip Mosley and the rest of our ilk. We even adopt them now.

On any Christmas Day in the 1970s predictably it would be Christmas dinner followed by The Queen's Speech, crackers pulled, wrapping paper cleared away, new toys everywhere and by seven o clock every arm chair taken and TV back on. The good old days when self regulated censorship still enabled whole families to sit down together and watch TV at its best with shows like Morecambe and Wise. Cleverly written scripts delivered by consummate professionals with innuendo subtle enough to fly over the heads of the youngest viewer, whilst giving the oldest the only exercise they may have taken that day – rocking with laughter. That's one of Stephen Tompkinson's earliest recollections, sitting on his grandad's knee to watch such shows, and loving it. 'As a child, I was impressed by things that made the grown-ups laugh, and those guys did.' Comedy fascinates him still from those beginnings with Grandad, Joseph Tompkinson, especially watching Morecambe and Wise and two more of his favourite classic comic actors of the past, Laurel and Hardy, whilst urging him to 'Watch Stan'.

Faith 2005

Stephen Tompkinson feels he became a Yorkshireman during the filming of Brassed Off. Photograph by kind permission of Nick Yates

'My other earliest memory is of my dad reading *Treasure Island* to me and my elder brother. You find yourself relating to different characters in it as you approach different stages in your life. Reading is massively important, because it offers that escapism and freedom to work with your imagination. You can be transported anywhere – it's limitless. In the times we live in it's great to be able to do that.'

Of course I had seen him before but only on screen as funny if amoral hack Damien Day in *Drop a Dead Donkey*, and stayed a fan when he had his hair cut and donned an Irish dog collar, became a wild at heart ex-pat, and grafted with a Geordie accent or when he did Shakespeare, original or with a Sally Wainwright skilful update. With a history still growing to this day solving crime is what we expect of him, though it was one dream come true for him to play opposite Helen Mirren in the final episode of *Prime Suspect*. That and worse to come *In Deep* put murder on his list and the true depth of his ability to chill an audience.

> 'People tend to know me for the variety of work I've done, which I'm delighted by. With the DCI Banks thing at the moment, I never smile but there are people who remember *Drop the Dead Donkey* and they recognise that.'

So when I first met him at the Calendar Girls' 10th Anniversary Gala with WB Yeats claim that if you give a man a mask he'll tell you the truth in mind, I wanted to know which of the masks was really his own. It's enough that he was unaffected, amiable, unassuming, genuinely interested in everything and everybody; and very bright. But it gets better when you begin to suspect that he might secretly have Yorkshire blood in his veins. He was that night made an Honorary Yorkshireman by Welcome to Yorkshire chief Gary Verity. Then there's his obsession with cricket, the fact that one of his best mates is Darren Gough and he rates filming *Brassed Off* as one of his favourites. In reality he tends to keep a low profile and appears in public or talks to the Press 'only when it is either about the work I am doing or an interview to help promote the work' but he readily agrees later to talk about playing the complex character of Phil in *Brassed Off*.

> 'Taking that role was one of the easiest decisions of my life. The man I play has the most dramatic journey of all and is difficult because he's not a character who earns sympathy. It's his own fault that his home life is such a mess as he doesn't communicate with his wife or his father and he ignores problems, but I still had to find some sympathy for him. The film's success is in part because of the music, but also because it could be about any small community facing such a crisis. It's a really powerful script in some cases about people who've almost thrown in the towel completely but also about this mining community, the grit, determination and the will to survive against the odds.'

What he omits to mention is the superb performances from start to finish in that film, including his own. But mention that film to anyone else who's seen it and they will instantly flash back to one of dozens of iconic moments. World Champion Grimethorpe Colliery Band, as it was then, is high on that list, but so is Tompkinson's searing depiction of a man's disintegration as he gradually learns that his father is dying, he is about to lose his job and that he has already lost his wife and the rest of his family. In the last scene of the Royal Albert Hall concert, watching his sick father's speech, Tompkinson's facial expression alone wins back an audience which has gradually grown away from the feckless, immature and insensitive character he had portrayed. It's a real-life watch Stan moment as Coco the Scab, with clown boots flapping over the edge of the stretcher, is wheeled along a hospital corridor. He regards himself as truly fortunate to have worked with Peter Postlethwite particularly in *Brassed Off* sharing some of his immersion techniques. I'm unsurprised to learn that whilst working on the film they became members of Grimethorpe Working Men's Club and spent their evenings there soaking up the atmosphere, but would be surprised if that was their sole reason. He is so passionately engaged in the culture that I assume, wrongly, that he has a mining background.

'There's no mining in the family, my mother Josephine was a junior school teacher, and my Dad Brian worked at the Yorkshire Bank. There is no history of acting in my family either. They quite rightly wanted me to do my A-levels and go to university.'

It was a great start to be in such a comfort zone of early learning and experience. He learnt the lessons he says his parents taught him, respect, to be grounded and to treat anyone whatever walk of life on their merits. With no clear ambition of taking up acting it was not until he was encouraged by an English teacher at High School:

'Mr Lynam, saw potential in me and asked me to audition for the annual nativity play which his wife wrote every year. He directed it as a comedy; I was the Innkeeper and loved it. He saw something in that performance which made him think that I could do well. By the time we did another Christmas show and then Dracula Spectacular I was totally hooked on acting.'

I had just seen him share centre-stage at the Royal Albert Hall in a star studded celebration of the Calendar Girls' Leukaemia Research fundraising at its best; with that same team approach he is as quick to recognise others' and credit their involvement in his own success:

> 'Jeff Lynam was a brilliant English teacher he inspired several other youngsters and directed in ways I understood completely; the kind of teacher you wanted to do well for. I took English language and literature at O-level and got an A in both and I'm as proud of Jeff as he is of me. He came when I was given an honorary fellowship from the University of Central Lancashire. He is inspirational I'm still in touch with him and if I'm doing a tour with a play nearby I always try to visit the school.'

Recalling that he 'got lucky again' at Sixth Form, St Mary's, in Blackpool where Stephen Brennan taught theatre studies and gave him a big first serious dramatic lead as John Proctor in *The Crucible*.

> 'Mum and dad came to see me and were so moved by it they said I could rip up their plans for university and go to drama school after A-levels if I still wanted to. So I owe a lot to Stephen Brennan as well.'

Accepted by the Central School of Speech and Drama in 1984, he found he had developed another passion, social injustice. It is with a genuine, residual but controlled anger that he recalls how much of his spare time he spent in the Kings Road with a bucket in his hand helping to boost collections in support of miners during that year long strike. It was nearly 30 years after that I met up with him, but the passion was still in his argument; now challenging the inequality of funding for the arts. Describing an 'amazing experience' to be amongst miners and other instrumentalists in the making of the Mark Herman's film he finds it incredible that the powers that be still do not appear to see what a travesty it would be to lose what was now a sponsor-less self-supporting Grimethorpe Brass Band.

> 'It's indication of how unfairly financial support is distributed across the Arts and yet another blow to a great community that's already had more than enough!'

This is a man who 30 minutes earlier was King Arthur, riding an imaginary horse on stage in the West End, with an audience aching with laughter. I think this is the real man though, charmingly straight to the point and genuinely asking how he can help a fundraising campaign to ensure that the most famous brass band in the world is not lost. He'll be back to Yorkshire on his own time, showing his parents' guidelines are still in play, and (even though he describes Richard the Third as 'a baddie' he'd really like to play) he really does deserve that Yorkshire badge.

Irrevocably breaking the black and white mould David Thacker's direction of *Faith* slices through type-casting presumptions with strength and weakness, right and wrong, conviction, fallibility and intransigence showing up in every character – just like the real world it portrays. Good and bad, manipulative or drifting, innocent or ignorant are deftly depicted by a single background shot, as twin TVs in a closed shop window simultaneously depict arguments from both political protagonists.

Pick your potential hero or villain as the messages fly unheeded over the heads of happily unaware leading characters who epitomise the people who will pay the real price. Complex relationships under the stress of one of the most painful of strikes in industrial history reveal human costs for political gain as women's strengths and weaknesses switch characters and sympathies shift. Simple subtleties carry similar caveats of judging motives for actions before understanding the reasons, not least in a portrayal of pickets turning their backs on a colleague who crosses the picket line. They are not reviling the man; it is silent support for an old workmate in a desperate situation at the end of his working life and at risk of losing his pension.

David Thacker is transparent about his stance when he first visited the area:

'Everyone has an outlook of one kind or another, I supported the miners but I was determined to keep an open mind in making the film. I was involved with a friend from Doncaster in making a theatre piece at the end of the strike for three weeks we meticulously recorded verbatim accounts of the behaviour of the police. Some we spoke to had even voted Tory in the past but were shocked and bewildered by the brutality and vandalism described they described to us.

Ordinary people with no political agenda showed us fridges which had been smashed for no reason; they were still shaken but

After filming Faith *David and Margot Thacker attended the Miners' Annual memorial lecture shown here with then NUM national & Yorkshire General Secretary Steve Kemp and his wife, Arthur Scargill and Lesley Hutchison.*

also outraged that the news was known to the rest of the outside world.

My hopes are with the young; they are the key to the future. They care about important things like saving the planet, about war, international events and about the big picture. That is where hope lies, with the young. They can and will change the world.'

He has a 'faith' in that hope, which I suppose can overcome residual resentment.

But if only Elizabeth Peacock been our first woman Prime Minister I suspect the outcome could have been very different, both then and now. As revealed later in her diary she was at least prepared to meet and discuss the situation with Arthur Scargill; at the cost of her parliamentary career. I suspect she could have done business with him or anyone else.

Had Michael Clark been Secretary of State for Trade and Industry a voice of reason might have prevailed rather than those who did call the tune.

Had David Moody been Lord Lieutenant of South Yorkshire then, his diplomatic skills and prior experience in the demise of an industry could been a very useful perspective. With an Oxford MA in Modern History he chose to begin his career in Yorkshire as a graduate apprentice at United Steels gaining experience of both private and public management there following its nationalisation. Promotion led to engagement in industrial relations but with simultaneous responsibility for production and sales. With that broad view of a wide range of needs and responsibilities he subsequently moved back to the private sector leading the first management buy out in the steel industry. In reminding me of the industry's own tough days when 90% of jobs had gone, he commends its recovery following similar government industrial restructuring decimation. His innumerable contributions since taking up office as Lord Lieutenant are too extensive to list here but include his ready support for the arts, the preservation of history, youth enterprise, communities, charities and churches including the 1st Miners' Memorial Service in Barnsley now in its 8th year and spreading county wide.

Similarly Sir John Alderson was one man whose experience and intellect could have enabled him to offer advice and philosophical professionalism to help resolve such mindset madness as that which prevailed in the 1980s. His advice, unwelcomed as it was by the then Prime Minister, could actually have pre-empted a great deal of the troubled outcomes of the 1984 strike. He understood not only the needs of the Government, but the interests of the establishment, the mood of the unions and the general public and he fought for a different approach. Advocating sound community policing rather than the imposition of what he regarded as enforced military colonial-type policing, the highly regarded once Chief Constable of Devon and Cornwall could only observe from a distance what he knew from his own childhood and education in the heart of the coalfield, was not 'the enemy within'. A boy soldier in the Highland Light Infantry, transferring to the Army Physical Training Corps he served in North Africa and Italy in World War Two. On discharge he joined the West Riding Constabulary where after only the statutory minimum nine years he attained the rank of Inspector and whilst also studying for a degree in law was promoted first to Chief Inspector, Subdivisional Commander and then Deputy Chief Constable of Dorset. His subsequent promotion if meteoric was well founded with a general respect never tainted by his own actions or those envious of it. His impeachable record and beneficial influence make him one of Barnsley's Registry of Births best kept secrets.

If only they had been in the team with integrity, skills, talent and enterprise, for the future which now again appears to show a need for coal as our own pits continue to be closed...

Chapter 13

The 1st Miners' Memorial Service

It was Lord Mason of Barnsley who first drew attention to the fact that Winston Churchill was right; miners should have had full and proper recognition for their part in the World War Two effort. It was 1943 when that idea was mooted and 1988 before it gained recognition in the House of Lords. It took a good deal of persistence and negotiation to achieve that end, but it was achieved and in itself was enough to motivate a group of likeminded people to renew that recognition. It also took a similar approach of negotiation, mutual support and cooperation to change that first idea into reality.

As Leader of Barnsley Council, Cllr Steve Houghton was a positive force in doing that.

His account of a miner's life growing up before 1992 is typical, 'Well lad you can be sure of two things...'

The words of retired miner Tommy Nixon, our next door neighbour, still echo in my mind,

'You'll get good training and you'll have a job for life.

I was off to start an apprenticeship with the Coal Board at Shafton Central Workshops, 'O' Levels clutched in hand. Sadly for me – and for thousands of others – the fullness of time would prove Tommy only half right.

It was 1974 and the second major strike in two years in the coal industry was over. The first, in 1972, gave me my first experience of industrial action. The school I attended had a series of closures due to lack of fuel and my father and I had to pick coal from the disused

159

railway embankment to keep our own fire burning. That was until people had burrowed so far in that the roof had collapsed and one young boy was killed. But in September 1974 the disputes were over and the future looked bright.

Mineworkers had better pay and conditions and something called pensions for the very first time. We also had the Labour Government's Plan for Coal securing energy supplies through coal fired power. I began work alongside four hundred and fifty other men. You learned to grow up fast.

Back in those days the coal industry was completely dominant in Barnsley. Jobs, houses, social services, sports leisure and further education were all supported through the production of coal. Those who didn't achieve in school got a second chance to learn and those who did often became the managers, union officials and local politicians. Whatever people did or didn't do at school there was always a job at the pit. Even in what was a relatively small private sector the focus was in supporting the National Coal Board.

We did have a history of glassmaking but the impact of coal was overwhelming. If there was a one horse town then we were it. But no matter we were immune from the volatility of private markets and the economy and whilst life wasn't significantly prosperous it was safe and secure. Notions of enterprise and entrepreneurship were alien concepts to us. Mining was a rules based industry to get you home safe and we became a rules based community as a consequence. The last thing you need down a coal mine is an entrepreneur. People then and now still find it difficult to understand how coal seeped through our veins and how dependant upon it we were; and how when the strike came and then when the pits closed, that dependency was cruelly exposed. Till then Barnsley was built upon three pillars – the Coal Board, the NUM and the Council – and we knew little else.

As Tommy forecast, my training was good as was the tutoring at Barnsley Technical College and four years later I emerged as a time served qualified electrician. Two years after that with an HNC in electrical and electronic engineering I was qualified to become an engineer. So what now? One thing the coal industry had was a culture of trade unionism – understandable given its history under private ownership – and I had been smitten. I began life with the local branch of the NUM.

The shift of emphasis was strongly influenced by the election of the Thatcher Government in 1979. A sense of unease was running through all of us. A future that once looked so bright was now in doubt. The Plan for Coal and long term energy planning was to be replaced by free markets, competition and privatisation. Energy production would be based upon cheap oil and gas, growing nuclear power and cheap coal imports. Planning for the future was no longer required and British Coal looked vulnerable. Pits would have to close. Equally there was a real sense that the Tories had a score to settle with the miners after their defeats in 1972 and 1974 and so we all began to prepare ourselves.

The next four years became something of a phoney war between the NUM and the Government and rhetoric was high. No pit closures was our rallying cry whilst the Government set about convincing the public that the country was in decline and it was all the fault of the Trade Unions. Equally the NUM predicted the destruction of jobs, lives and communities if pit closures went ahead. The scene was being set. Rather than take on the miners straight away the Government set about re-structuring and privatising other public industries. Inevitably disputes followed.

The decimation of the steel industry was a particular blow to us. Not only had steel and coal a long history together both economically and socially they were also two in not the two big trade union battalions and the steel workers were defeated. It also reduced the demand for coking coal dramatically weakening our economic position even further.

At the same time the Government set our reforming the industrial relations landscape – particularly the rules on secondary picketing. Coupled with increasing coal stocks and the increase in the number of alternative fuels we were being emasculated and we could do nothing to prevent it. Indeed the Government even had the chance to test their new methods and the police to train for them. The print disputes at Warrington (which I witnessed first hand) and Grunwick brought a new legislative and policy approach to striking workers not previously seen. So by the time 1984 came round the Government was ready – but we weren't deterred. We weren't going to see our way of life destroyed on the back of some right wing ideology and not without a fight. They had the power of the state but we had our sense of community and our sense of right. We were sure our fight would galvanise the whole Trade Union and Labour movement into action.

When the strike came it began not in Barnsley but in Rotherham at Cortonwood Colliery. The shout of 'No pit closures' went up. It wasn't long before we were on a bus to Markham Main Colliery in Derbyshire. I was a flying picket! A freezing February night was followed by a minor victory of sorts. The early shift arrived but Derbyshire men went home in sympathy and we went home to sleep. It would be a similar pattern for the next few months. But why were we challenging our own? There had as yet been no national ballot for strike action.

Yorkshire had done so many months before in expectation of what was to come. The argument went – a national ballot would mean those in areas free from pit closures deciding whether those under threat should go on strike – and we weren't having that. We expected our plight to be supported by others in their own areas and one by one each region voted to come out with one major exception Nottinghamshire. We also expected the wider movement and the Labour Party to follow suit and line up behind us. The absence of that national mandate didn't seem to matter at the time but as things progressed it meant division within our ranks and support from the wider movement failing to materialise. It would prove to be our undoing. Nonetheless we were up and running and we attempted to disrupt production in the Nottinghamshire coalfield.

The police had other ideas. Police forces from all over the country now converged on mining communities in their thousands. Motorways were either regulated or secured off – roads and streets were blocked and people's movements restricted. Our communities were being occupied. We pressed on nonetheless.

My first visit to Nottingham was to Babington Colliery near the city. Despite police efforts we arrived and found our way onto a large grass bank with lots of largely good natured heckling and shouting. We were there in our hundreds and so were the police. When the local miners went into work there was what was to be the usual booing and jeering. But then something different; snatch squads. Inexplicably when people were ready to leave squads of officers cut deep into the strikers ranks to pick out and arrest particular individuals seemingly without reason. If people had behaved badly then action was expected, but to snatch people at random without just cause was something new, and as far as we were concerned something sinister. It set a tone.

We spent the coming months of the strike taking the struggle to the Nottinghamshire pits. Howarth, Hucknall, Ollerton, Clipstone, Bilsthorpe, Cotgrave and many more. At one point we were allocated Rufford – looked at the map and set off for Lancashire. We were going the wrong way – who says we were well organised. At one point we attended a rally in Mansfield and ended up occupying the Nottinghamshire NUM Headquarters. Strikers on one side, working miners on the other. The enmity between the two sides was palpable. At the same time the Police lockdown deepened. Stress increased. Tempers frayed and behaviour began to deteriorate on all sides. All major road networks were now closed off and anyone remotely looking like a miner or working man was being stopped and turned away. Protesting would only get you arrested. We didn't give up. We came to know every road, path, track and footpath into Nottinghamshire and we changed our appearance. Out went jeans and trainers; in came collars, ties and briefcases. Many of us still got through but the numbers were decreasing. The summer weather was glorious but our impact was not. A sense of frustrations began to grow.

The strike was the centre of national conversation. Was it right? How long would it last? Would it succeed? What's happening in the talks with the employers and Government? How long would we be expected to go on? Can we get help with unpaid mortgages and bills? It was also being debated amongst miners and their families and at local NUM branch meetings. Ours were on Saturday mornings at Shafton Working Men's Club. We would report on events, discuss next week's picketing and distribute food parcels and vouchers to those in most need.

In the early days optimism and enthusiasm was high. Six months in the hurt began to show. The soup kitchens were full. For my part I was fortunate, a single man with no commitments. The car went as did the savings but I had my parents to fall back on. Others weren't so lucky. Family men and women had debts to pay and children to look after. How much could we expect from them? How much had we a right to expect from them? By late summer people were questioning the union's methods. Could we slow coal production enough to hurt the Government and the economy?

Tactics increasingly moved towards single mass pickets – the ultimate being the Orgreave coking plant. Much has been said about Orgreave but one thing was certain we and the Government knew it would be a turning point. And so it proved. Despite every effort the plant remained open in production. Not only did public opinion start to believe the strike would fail so did many of those involved. Both before and after Orgreave questions were raised about behaviour and tactics of striking miners and there were clearly actions by some which were both wrong and regrettable. But many of those took place in a context where policing by consent disappeared. Where external forces came not to police the strike but to break it, they did so in some instances quite brutally. Police officers waving five and ten pound notes at hungry strikers only increased tensions and bitterness.

Ironically South Yorkshire Police also became victims of these events. The behaviour of those external forces left a legacy of mistrust between the police and the local communities which took years to put right.

So as autumn came men in coalfields which had previously stayed solid with the strike began to return to work. Our fight was no longer elsewhere but now in our own backyard and the bitterness and sense of betrayal towards those working was immense. The picket lines were now in Yorkshire. We went to Brodsworth, en masse. To force a way through the Police were literally driving vans through the picket lines – people were scattered everywhere – it was chaos. This is bound to make the news tonight I thought, the public will be appalled. They were, but not with the Police but with the IRA. It was the day of the Brighton bomb. Then hope. Talk of a settlement around October time. Spirits were raised and then dashed. The discussions came to nought. The drift back which had first slowed then grew.

There was a rally in Barnsley to raise our spirits. Rodney Bickerstaff, head of the National Union of Public Employees, was the main speaker. A brilliant socialist and orator, he entertained as well as inspired. We had a drink afterwards in the Royal Hotel. 'How's it going?' he asked. I expressed doubts. 'Well you're a miserable bugger' he said. We laughed but the doubts remained.

As Christmas approached the long hot summer was a distant memory as the cold set in. Branch meetings became fraught. People were hurting and could see no way out. Talk was of going back to work. Families once loyal had had enough. We pleaded, begged, persuaded and warned. The strike was bound to end soon, why go back now with all the bitterness and revulsion it would bring? It worked for a while but not for long. Soon we were picketing our own colleagues, some of whom had stood side by side with us only months earlier. Is a man who spends 10 months on strike, loses his home, even his family to be blackened because he can take no more? In the emotion of the time I was sure, I am no longer. The dispute dragged on until February. We voted to return to work. We were beaten. Yet the sense of pride in our struggle never left us. We believed our cause was just – I still do.

How did we manage to stay out for so long with the might of the state against us? The support of miner's wives and families was crucial. The Women Against Pit Closures movement inspired and politicised a whole new generation. Now there was politics at the breakfast table where it hadn't been before. Above all our struggle for justice, and our community spirit got us through. It also enabled us to return to work with our dignity when the day finally came.

Back at work the repercussions were swift. A pit closure programme was announced as were changes to how the industry would work. Miner against miner in the strike was exchanged for pit against pit in a battle for profitability. Between 1985 and 1993 the coal industry disappeared in Barnsley. Our reason for being went with it. We not only lost our economy we lost our purpose. Over 20,000 mining jobs disappeared. Economists calculated a similar number outside the industry went with them. Unemployment, crime and deprivation rocketed, as did the bitterness. The NUM's predictions had come true. The Tory Government did nothing. We were told the market and the private sector would step in to fill the gap. It didn't.

As for miners themselves it was a mixed picture. Those craftsmen with transferable skills often relocated and found work. But for the majority it was redundancy and early retirement or a life on Incapacity Benefit. The Government turned a blind eye to sympathetic doctors signing men into the benefits system. It kept the unemployment figures down. But it left us with a growing culture of despair and worklessness we still have today almost three generations later. By 1993 two of Barnsley's three pillars had been destroyed and I was left to the Council with help from Europe to try to pick up the pieces. Ironically at the same time the Government under John Major decided to cut public expenditure. The challenge became even bigger.

Somehow we have managed to get through. The return of a Labour Government in 1997 brought significant investment but is has taken 25 years to return our economy to the levels of 1985. During that time generations have been lost and potential left unfulfilled. Consequently the change process we have gone through has not been easy. The greatest strength of our Borough, its sense of community which did so much to sustain the strike, has also proved to be its greatest weakness. Change has not come easily as dependency on the state has grown not reduced as a consequence of pit closures. The lack of an enterprising and learning culture which meant so little during the days of coal became our Achilles heel. It took a long time for our communities to start looking forward and not back.

And for me? My job was lost in 1993. My last 19 years have been spent on the Council trying to repair the damage and restore our purpose. However, whilst I have learned the hard way, change is inevitable, governments have not yet learned about the need to manage change, its impact, or its consequences. We now face another battle for our public services and our new economy with ministerial rhetoric similar to that of before – the markets and the private sector will provide.

De ja vu.

But whatever challenges we face in the future we will have a sense of pride and a sense of history that we played our part in defending our communities and a way of life we will never have again.'

In was in 2006 that it was suggested that a service to commemorate all those who had died working in the coal or related industries would be appropriate. A working group was quickly set up chaired by the then Yorkshire area NUM Secretary Steve Kemp and consisting of the Rev Ian Wiley then Canon of St Mary's Church, Ken Capstick and Phil Thompson of the NUM and myself. After a few weeks of massive support and delicate negotiations the first such service took place in at St Mary's Church, Barnsley.

National Union of Mineworkers
(Yorkshire Area)

in conjunction with
St Mary's Church, Barnsley & Barnsley MBC

Invite you to a

MINERS' MEMORIAL DAY SERVICE

to be held on SUNDAY 1st OCTOBER 2006

at ST. MARY'S CHURCH, BARNSLEY

at 11 A.M.

(Followed by food & concert at Barnsley Town Hall
with MALTBY MINERS' WELFARE BAND)

The introduction to the presentation by children was led by the Bishop of Wakefield Stephen Platten:

'After I arrived here in 2003 I was asked to speak at the NUM miners' memorial service in St Mary's Barnsley. I knew it would be a powerful experience for me for three or four quite different reasons. First of all I had married into a family, much of whose lives had been fashioned and moulded by the experience of coal mining in the north east of England. My father-in-law had been an electrician at Woodhorn and Ashington pits and his brother-in-law moved from being under-manager at Lynemouth Colliery eventually to becoming Deputy Director of Industrial Training with the National Coal Board. As if that was not sufficient, my own first descent into a colliery was in 1974 at Frickley/South Elmsall Colliery even within the bounds of this Diocese of Wakefield! For a lily-livered southerner from the further outskirts of North London this was a most powerful experience. Only a few days earlier I had seen the blast furnace tapped at Park Gate steelworks in Sheffield and these two experiences in such swift succession to each other changed my entire understanding of social issues.

Barnsley is a very special place in all this. Indeed the South Yorkshire coalfield had been one of the most productive in England along with Nottinghamshire and it is not surprising that in the strike in the 1980s these were some of the places where the sharpest exchanges occur and where the deepest scars have been left. For all these reasons the service in St Mary's was particularly powerful. Only fairly recently before that I had found out about the famous and tragic Huskar Pit disaster in the mid-nineteenth century. Occurring in 1838, twenty-six children were killed. Those sorts of tragedies remind us of the extraordinarily tough nature of the mining industry, but they also remind us of the remarkable community spirit which was generated by the industry. One of the further tragedies, following the strike and the collapse of deep mining in England has been the loss of community.

All of these feelings and issues were raised powerfully in that service in St Mary's those years ago. We began with music from the Maltby Miner's Band. That whole tradition of brass bands has also been so important in supporting community spirit. We saw that all so powerfully in the film *Brassed Off* which portrayed a very thinly disguised Grimethorpe. One of the greatest pities is the severing of the links of the great brass bands of northern England from the coalmines and woollen mills which originally prospered them. In that service in 2006, the Mayor of Barnsley Cllr Margaret Morgan then moved us into the next phase and introduced a particularly poignant performance by children from St Mary's primary School and the Lamproom Theatre with local folk musician Dick Walker. twenty-six children then laid flowers in memory of all the miners who had lost their lives in the mining industry. That reminded us particularly of the tragedies nearby to Barnsley itself, and specifically that at Huskar. With more music following (this time *Jerusalem*) from the Maltby Band, and after this Steve Kemp, the NUM National and Yorkshire Area Secretary spoke. It was powerful to have such a senior union official as NUM National President Ian Lavery with us. Following this came the miners' hymn *Gresford* played by the band once again, after which wreaths were laid.

Lord Lieutenant of South Yorkshire and The Mayor of Barnsley Cllr Margaret Morgan laid the first wreaths. Photograph by kind permission of Tim Dyke

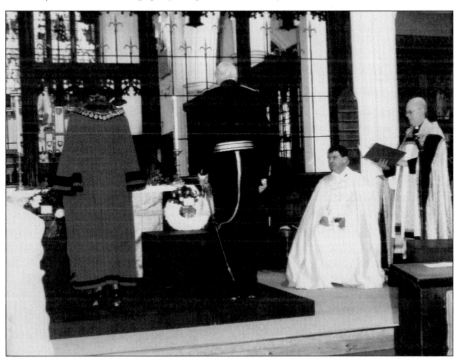

I then offered some reflections myself picking up some of the links I have already mentioned. I pointed out how in going down into Caphouse Colliery at the nearby National Coal Mining Museum one experiences something which is safe, dry, light, cool and clean. Almost all those adjectives are the exact opposites of what one normally experiences in a pit. I have now been down some 7 or 8 times (twice recently at Kellingley, where once again only two years ago two lives were lost). When you descend into the main workings of a colliery you find yourself in a damp, hot (up to 35°C), dusty and noisy environment. Nevertheless alongside this runs an extraordinary rhythm of humour and camaraderie which stood at the heart of those communities I mentioned earlier.

I also mentioned that a number of the early Labour party campaigners issued from the interesting confluence of 'mining and Methodism'. I noted that probably the most important of the beatitudes in the Sermon on the Mount for them was 'blessed are those who hunger and thirst for righteousness' and 'blessed are those who are persecuted for righteousness' sake, for theirs is the kingdom of heaven.' Not only did they generate political awareness and a religious response, but also they produced some of the greatest sportsmen of their generation. Ashington, where my father-in-law had been an electrician was the birthplace of Bobbie and Jackie Charlton and Jackie Milburn. Slightly less recently the 'Pitmen Painters', working just before and during the Second World War, were part of the community in Ashington. Not only has there been an exhibition of their work and a book illustrating this, but more recently there has appeared a play which has taken the West End of London by storm.

Ever since that service which I remember so well, much has happened in the mining industry. We are just about to lose Maltby although we are told that perhaps one or two other pits may be brought back to life. Kellingley continues and produces a lot of coal. Although our world has moved on, we should never lose track of the tradition and indeed the contribution that has been offered from the deep mining of coal in this country – nowhere else has that been more sharply marked than in the South Yorkshire Coalfield and based largely on the town of Barnsley which itself has been a quarry for so much talent in a variety of worlds and not forgetting literature in so many different forms.'

The 1st Miners' Memorial Service

On Sunday 21 October 2012, in the Minster Church of St George, Doncaster, the Right Reverend Peter Burrows gave the blessing at the 7th Miners' Memorial Service:

'Over the past few months as I've settled into my post as the Bishop of Doncaster, it's been an education to listen to humbling stories and history told by ex-miners and their families about life down the pit and living in the mining communities. I can only imagine how hard the work was and I certainly don't have the courage or bravery to work in the conditions that so many miners did and still, in places, do. I also know that to dedicated, hardworking and close knit communities the closure of so many pits over the years has left them devastated. The loss of community, the stability and identity the mining community provided, the working spirit passed on from one generation to another, is now for many a cherished memory. Though I've also come to appreciate and value the resilience of the mining communities as they've learnt to move on and adapt as much as they are able.

But the memories are important and cherished because they remind us how much the mining community contributed to our country and economy. They also recall the thousands of miners who lost their lives in the collieries or through related diseases from working down the mines.'

As has become the custom children continue to be involved, and their considered inputs are directed to reflect the specific losses in the area in which the service is hosted. 2012's excellent presentation by the Yew Tree Theatre Group was followed by Chris Skidmore, Yorkshire Area NUM Chairman's moving address:

'Everyone remembers the loss of life in the sinking of the *Titanic*. Historical narratives will also mention that 1912 saw Sir Robert Scott reach the South Pole, sadly never to return: that the first parachutist dropped out of the sky from a moving aeroplane: Barnsley won the English FA Cup for the first time: But more importantly, what isn't said is that Cadeby Main Colliery was rocked by two underground explosions.

The particularly terrible loss of life at Cadeby Main Colliery between Doncaster and Rotherham saw ninety one men and boys lose their lives. This happened to coincide with a visit to the area by the then King and Queen who themselves were devastated by the news and demanded to return to the village to give their own support to the bereaved.

Likewise in the pit village of Bentley, two tragedies befell that community, one in November 1931 so wonderfully and movingly portrayed by the Yew Tree Theatre Group today, where forty five lives were lost in another explosion and again in November 1978 where a further seven men were killed in a paddy train accident. It is worth noting that the highest award for bravery recognised as a British civilian decoration is the Edward Medal. Instituted in July 1907 by Royal Warrant, it recognises acts of bravery by miners and quarrymen, and that a total of fourteen were awarded for heroism in the Cadeby Main Colliery and first Bentley Pit disasters.

I recently attended another commemoration at Allerton Bywater near Leeds, where I spoke about celebrating a way of life, of friendships forged at work, about the sense of pride, of watching out for each other, of respect earned in the community as well as at work and to be able to laugh and cry when the occasion demands, because to quote a few words from a poem by Scottish miner J H Smith: "It's in the blood".

Let's not forget the positive impact of the miners in our communities. The interest in sport, the Miners' Welfare facilities, the Reading Rooms, the allotment societies, fishing clubs, pigeon and caged bird societies, the art work and the humour. Miners have always encouraged their children to read and write and to endeavour to aspire to a good standard of education. Most of the pits have now gone and a generation of children have not had jobs in the pit but it is only right and proper that we remember the efforts of those who have gone before, as well as those still with us who have given their working lives to the mines.'

As had been Steve Kemp's and my hope that it would become an annual event, when we were informed that the Leader of Rotherham Council, Roger Stone, was so moved by the event he was determined that his local authority would host a similar service the following year, the NUM immediately supported that and has continued to do so ever since. In September 2006, Jeff Ennis Member of Parliament for Barnsley East tabled the following motion in the House of Commons:

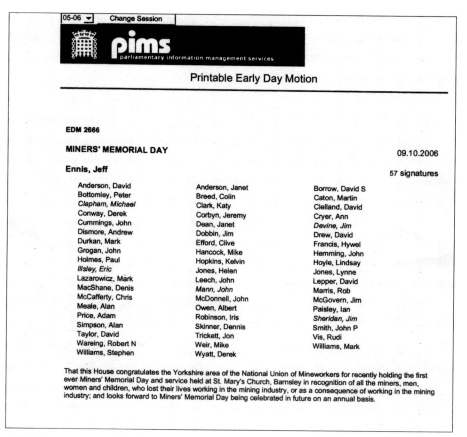

Official recognition of the first Memorial Day for those who died serving their country as a result of working in mining.

On Sunday 7 October 2007 the second service did take place in Rotherham Minster.

In 2008 Sheffield took up the practice, then 2009 Wakefield, followed by Selby Abbey in 2010, 2011 at St Giles Pontefract and in 2012 in Doncaster Minster.

In 2013 the service will take us back to Barnsley.

Chapter 14

Finale or Future

Asked by a colleague if I would be willing to present the awards at the school to which she had just been appointed as Deputy Head, I agreed. Some months later I heard that the invitation had been withdrawn as the school was 'forward looking' and did not wish to 'dwell on the past history of the area in which it was situated.' I disagree. The elephant in that room is that whether they hear about it in school or at home most children are aware of their family history, frequently enjoy finding out about it and I believe should be encourage to celebrate it. It was increasingly clear to me in collating this material and listening to those whose contributions form the major part of this book, that for them the past remains as important as the future.

Bishop Nigel McCulloch at the time of writing Her Majesty's Lord High Almoner and Bishop of Manchester also sees importance of the past as a prerequisite for accepting change:

> 'How long ago those days seem now. Twenty years have seen huge changes – some for the better, some for the worse. But now, thanks to Mel, some of the tales of those frightening times and the private memories, and the personal joys and sorrows, will never be forgotten. I thank God for the honour of playing a tiny role in one particular part of Grimethorpe's history – and for the privilege I was given of being alongside some lovely and brave people in a time of need.'

In that time of need and following the invaluable support of the Coalfields Community Campaign throughout the early 90s it was also a relief to many in 1999 to see that something would remain of that organisation. Susanne Bell reassures me,

'That the Charitable Company the Coalfields Regeneration Trust was set up dedicated to improving the quality of life in Britain's coalfield communities through social enterprise and delivery of services and programmes which will make a positive difference. Ensuring resources would be targeted to areas in greatest need, delivering new models for social enterprise to achieve financial independence and working collaboratively with stakeholders to maximise the value of investments are priorities bringing real improvements efficiently and effectively maintained hope towards regeneration of the area.'

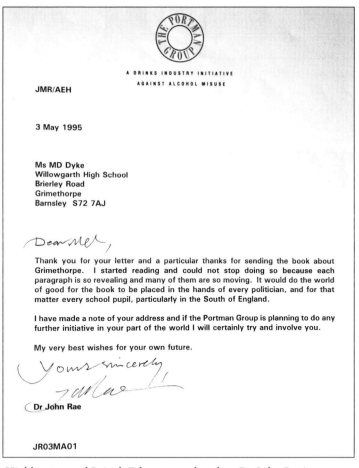

Highly esteemed British Educator and author, Dr John Rae's own record as Head Master of Westminster School, makes this response praise indeed.

Susanne Bell continues,

'The vision is that those communities will again become sustainable, prosperous, viable and cohesive without support, so able to bring back strong prosperous communities with high aspirations, work opportunities to use their available new skills and qualifications. These will be places where families feel supported and have good access to local services which are supportive to the needs of children and young people to help them achieve their full potential. Creativity in tackling health issues, moving people to engage in healthy lifestyle activities are encouraged to maximise pride in their local identity whilst interacting with the infrastructure to nurture new businesses and social enterprise. Achievement of these objectives looks to bring solutions around poverty issues in some of the most disadvantaged communities in the land, working with the financial inclusion sector. Sixty community apprenticeships for young people and investment in initiatives are set to assist in the development of social enterprise. In short, giving back to the communities in these areas the dignity and lifestyles they once enjoyed.'

Rodney Bickerstaffe would not for one second agree with the – 'let's forget it!' approach. Looking back to the struggle of 1992–93, one of his revived memories is taking part in writing a book in a day:

'A book in a day about a crime of the century!
During the final defence against the Tory government's siege of its own people, our country's mining villages, this idea, this event gave focus and heart to a proud South Yorkshire community.
A spirited collective will, huge effort and a refusal to be crushed without leaving some cultural remembrance; this was no "magnus opus" from the pen of an incoming observer. It was and is about the voices of many in 1992, repeating the whispers down the years: "Yes a battle lost. Yet not this day, but one day – the war will be won by our kind.'

Also noting similarities between his own military experience and possibly in light of the fact that these are the people who were once called 'the enemy within', Member of Parliament for Barnsley Central Dan Jarvis' stance is:

Even Rodney Bickerstaffe's famed negotiation skills were at times stretched... Photograph by kind permission of Rodney Bickerstaffe.

'Across Yorkshire and in Barnsley, mining has been the fibre that has linked families, created friendships and is what many of our communities were built on – communities built on coal. Barnsley is a town synonymous with the mining industry. It brought families together, giving them homes, jobs and livelihoods. It is our history and it has shaped our future. I believe we should be very proud of our mining heritage and what it has brought to our region.

My early memories of mining are vivid. I grew up in Margaret Thatcher's Britain. I remember what a terrible place it was; the rich in the South getting richer, at the expense of people like the mineworkers of Barnsley. I have often heard it described as the government declaring civil war on its own people, cutting off their income and forcing them to give in due to near starvation and poverty. It was a government that wielded its power and would make sure they won at any cost. This was not just about workers rights; this was about the civil rights of the people in coalfield communities – communities that depended on the pit for the local economy to thrive. In Barnsley, we still bear the scars. Some of these scars will linger for generations to come, no matter how much regeneration and investment is brought in to help the economic recovery of the local area, where there is still an enormous reserve of coal under the ground.

Mining communities are incredibly resilient. The community spirit in the former minefield areas is among the strongest I have ever known. This is borne out of the principles of people working, living closely and sticking together, through thick and thin. The camaraderie that the men developed underground, when they knew their lives could be in one another's hands, transcended from the confines of the pit below to the community above. Throughout the years, miners and their families have supported one another through the toughest of times, sharing their resources and doing it all in the steadfast belief that they were stronger when united, more formidable when as one.

This is particularly true of the miners' fight for a decent wage and to improve the conditions they worked in – only possible through collective action and mass representation. Miners stood shoulder to shoulder and fought – they did not roll over and fall at the first hurdle. They withstood severe hardship and poverty, in order to stand up for the principles that were ingrained in their hearts. Throughout the region today, the memories of many people still bear testament to the fight that miners across the country had to take on in the 1980s in order to protect their welfare and their way of life.

Among the most impressive groups in the struggle were the inspirational women of Barnsley; the *Women Against Pit Closures*. This was an incredible collective of women who were determined to fight and support all who were struggling as a result of the strike. The role they played in the Miners' Strike cannot be underestimated – the strike simply could not have continued without their unwavering support.

As a former soldier, I recognise the many similarities between the duties and camaraderie that exists between soldiers on active service and that which is so evident among coal miners. They are both public servants, yet their work is not carried out in a public arena. Whether in the deserts of Africa or the pitch black tunnels underground, they worked for the people of the UK. They

Dan Jarvis MP for Barnsley Central on first visit to the NUM's annual Memorial lecture in Barnsley shortly after taking his seat in Parliament.

experience a shared hardship, a common goal. Above all, they depend on one another. Both roles are incredibly demanding and come with immense danger. The death toll among miners was extraordinary, with individual disasters claiming hundreds of lives.

Today, there are just fifteen underground coal mines in the UK. Of those, just a few are in Yorkshire. Despite this, many communities in the region still uphold the values that were so heavily entrenched within them from when the British mining industry was in its prime. Whilst Barnsley is now a different place, we must be proud of our history, proud of our mining heritage and proud of the people who fought over the years to keep this town alive. After all, mining was not just a job. It was – and is – a way of life.'

Connections between mining and military service seem more evident in the recent past as the lack of career opportunities in mining may be linked to enlistment in the armed forces. Recognition of The Light Dragoons' Regimental history is located at the Cannon Hall Museum and The Yorkshire Regiment which has a 'History and Home' theme in its recruitment and both regiments have recently been awarded Freedom of the Borough. Barnsley's three degrees of separation immediately conjures up the battleground of North Africa, not unfamiliar to Egyptologist Dr Joann Fletcher.

Her successes are not confined to PhD expertise in the matter of ancient Egyptian adornment and hairstyles, or the identification of former Pharaohs, or her twenty five year's research leading to recognition of Barnsley-born gifted artist Harold Jones' contribution to archaeology. First revelation of that was in her 2012 appearance at the Cooper Gallery's annual Sadler lecture named in recognition of yet another Barnsley great. The gallery's first ever sold out lecture delivery brought her universal accolades from the youngest twelve-year-old pupils of Horizon and Darton Colleges to the Lord Lieutenant's appreciation of her scholastic knowledge and engaging passion for her subject. Nor is she a limelight seeker despite her high profile involvement in and presentation of televisual revelations of the recent ground breaking reconstruction of the mummification process

Dr Joann Fletcher: her face concealed behind the BAFTA she helped win.
Photograph by kind permission of Dr Stephen Buckley.

Joann Fletcher with Beattie Squires, returns to meet up with her favourite Barnsley Sunday School teacher and long term friend of her mother.

together with her partner Dr Stephen Buckley: as her absence from the actual BAFTA winners ceremony would indicate, though she did later catch up with the award.

Her circle is completed when she reminds me of her family history. Her great grandparents, Herbert and Janet Fletcher ran a hairdressing business in Birdwell for years. Her Aunt Julie was for many a hairdresser in Lesley Frances' salon in Barnsley – a national and internationally recognised 'leading hair salon', she rightly reminds me. And her maternal grandfather Horace Hayes worked in mining, not as a face or surface worker, but as a member of, and then Chief of, the essential Mines Rescue Service stationed at Barnsley Main Colliery. So her total loyalty to the town through inestimable her Arts in Action input in its schools, colleges and adult groups from ages three to ninety-three, is not mere nostalgia, it's in the blood. The unsurpassed variety and depth of her experience in these fields as its consultant archaeologist ensures a quality of expertise which

Miners' Rescue Team member Horace Hayes front row left was Joann Fletcher's grandfather.
Photograph by kind permission of Barnsley Chronicle

Experience Barnsley could otherwise not have dreamed of without her contributions. One of the prime concerns in opening part of Barnsley Town Hall to the people of Barnsley as a living heritage centre complete with an archive, museum with a recording studio facility was to ensure that the town's recorded and oral history and heritage could be fully recognised and not forgotten.

The original suggestion for that history in voices came from historian Brian Elliott as did displaying the town's varied development in a worldwide timeline across the centuries. His series of *Aspects of Barnsley* over years of carefully researched and recorded work does just that. But it is his inspired collection of recorded veteran miners' voices which accompanied his 2005 publication *Yorkshire Mining Veterans* which will take those stories into the town's audio archive to inspire others to visit and include their own history for children and adults for ears in years to come.

Michael Dugher MP has been Member of Parliament for Barnsley east since 2012. He is also Vice-Chair of the Labour Party, reflects on his childhood in the coalfields:

'I grew up about ten miles from the edge of what is today my Barnsley East constituency. I was raised in a village called Edlington, which was for many years the home of the Yorkshire Main Colliery. Edlington is about 15 miles from Grimethorpe and the two communities, even to this day, look similar. As was the case for many families in Grimethorpe, my grandmother's family had originally come to Edlington because they were looking for work in the South Yorkshire coalfield. Her family settled in Edlington and indeed helped to sink the Yorkshire Main pit more than a century ago.

Michael Dugher, Labour Member of Parliament for Barnsley East. Photograph by kind permission of Michael Dugher MP

My father wasn't a miner. Like most of the men on his side of the family, my Dad worked on the railways. But the house that I grew up was on Markham Road, the backdoor to which looked out onto the pit. I remember as a kid looking out at the pit wheel and the main building of the colliery. My brother and I played football alongside the nearby colliery fence. Every year we watched the

Miners' Gala in the village. I remember my Dad, who played for the Yorkshire Main colliery cricket team, teaching me to ride my bike on the track that ran round the cricket pitch at the Miners' Welfare. In so many ways the pit formed the backdrop to childhood.

But it was the strike, and then ultimately the closure of the pit, that probably had the most dramatic impact of my early political development too. I remember the police, many on horse-back, being deployed on the streets during the strike. School trips and our weekly swimming lessons were cancelled. Most of my classmates were on free school meals. As a nine-year-old boy in 1984, I also discovered that a "scab" was something other than what you got if you fell over and cut your knee. And rather than government being a concept 'of the people, by the people, for the people'; government instead was seen in our community as being completely hostile to its own people.

In the spring of 1985, I vividly remember being late for school as my friend, Gavin Ward (whose father worked down the pit), and I marched with the local National Union of Mineworkers as the men returned to work. The Yorkshire Main, like so many other pits, was closed shortly afterwards.

It is impossible to underestimate the trauma that the strike and the subsequent pit closure programme had on areas like Edlington in the mid-eighties or Grimethorpe later in the early 1990s. Virtually the entire economic system that supported those villages was gone, pretty much overnight. Poverty increased and unemployment rocketed. Many men would never work again. Some became self-employed, others eventually got jobs (often more badly paid and less satisfying) in nearby factories, some people simply moved away. But the pits also supported the social infrastructure of those communities too – from village sport to the brass band.

I remember when I first heard the news in 1992 about the Government's pit closure programme that went on to hit places like Grimethorpe. I was at sixth form at the time, studying for my 'A' levels and hoping to go to university. I was studying politics, but in many ways you only had to switch on the TV to see what politics meant to your own neighbourhood. The euphoria that we experienced with the resignation of Margaret Thatcher in 1990 had long since been overtaken by depression, as we saw Labour lose the 1992 general election to the Conservatives.

Just six months after that electoral defeat in 1992, I watched the BBC News bulletin as it was announced that the then-Conservative government planned to close a third of Britain's deep coal mines, with an estimated loss of 31,000 jobs. I remember people saying at the time that what the NUM had warned about all those years before – that the Tories had a secret plan to close down the British coal industry – was finally coming true. By March 1993, only 19 pits were left.

I am a big believer that you have to remember where you came from. Our industrial heritage in South Yorkshire is incredibly important. Not just because we should pay tribute to the people who built our communities – those brave men and women who worked long, dangerous hours and in an industry that powered Britain's industrial revolution. That is why things like 'Experience Barnsley', the new museum, are so important.

But the truth is it's important to think about the past because many of the virtues and the values of those mining communities are still as relevant today: like a belief in hard work; in the importance of community and the need to take pride in it; about togetherness, solidarity and honouring the duties that we owe one another.

Places like Edlington or Grimethorpe are rightly proud of their past. It's the job of historians to keep those memories alive, to be cherished for future generations. But it's the job of us politicians to ensure that young people growing up in those communities today have the decent opportunities to work and to live in the future. The pits may have gone, but those communities are still very much alive.'

Kate Dalton is one of those young people Michael Dugher talks about; brought up and educated in Grimethorpe throughout the troubled times of the 1990s. She is also able to answer a question posed by Chrissie Yates currently Assistant Principal Human Resources, Minsthorpe Community College – which by coincidence was an Alec Clegg flagship school and formally opened by HRH The Duke of Edinburgh:

'Having shared a converted corridor at Longcar PDC with the indomitable Mel Dyke, when I got the call from her to go to Grimethorpe to deliver a session on Equality in terms of gender and choices, it was an opportunity I wouldn't have missed for the world.

It was 1990 and Mel and I had worked together the previous year under the TVEI umbrella. Mel was Advisory Teacher for SEN & Inclusion and I with one other colleague, was Advisory Teacher for Equal Opportunities, Gender and Ethnicity. They were heady days that were full of promise and opportunities and a real commitment in certain educational areas to raise the awareness of the issues so many of our young people experienced (and sadly still do) in terms of the choices they had and what they could aspire to be. Feminism was a misunderstood term; almost a dirty word in those days, few realising that the term equated to the notion of choices for all despite your social class, gender or ethnicity.

Willowgarth High School that day was buzzing and humming! The calibre of women invited in was a "Who's who" of vibrant women who were making a difference in their chosen fields. Boys and girls from families which had had little hope for generations were having the blinkers taken from their eyes with opportunities and ideas being presented to them in a barrage of excitement and an ethos of "You can do it too!"

Laptops and PowerPoints hadn't really taken off in those days. It was leading and talking by example; it was questioning and raising issues, awareness and asking questions. It was fabulous!

I felt we were on the cusp of something extraordinary and maybe we were.

I believe many young women of today need to thank the women that did what we did at a time when it was the norm to be misunderstood and patronised; to be accused of a left wing feminist agenda that had no place in our schools. I would love to know if we touched anyone and could quantify the difference a day in a school in Grimethorpe may have made to all who attended in whatever guise.'

Now Kate Dalton recalls those days from far afield:

'I remember being part of a group of Willowgarth students who were interviewed by Radio Sheffield. We were asked what opportunities we thought might be available to us in Barnsley now that the mines were closed and there was an economic downturn. We all gave the answer that we thought was the correct thing to say – that it was important to pass our exams so we could have good qualifications

Mick Clapham MP, Kate Dalton, Julia Utley and Eric Illsley MP in the 1995 visit to Westminster.

and secure jobs. I think we mostly believed what we were saying. The interviewer asked me about my uncle (an ex-miner) who had just been employed as a caretaker at Willowgarth. She was trying to use him as the light-hearted upbeat final point; an example that it was not all doom and gloom for the students of Grimethorpe. I think it was then that I realized how low hopes were for us if my highly skilled, ex-mine engineer uncle was now being congratulated for landing a caretaking job.

Looking back now it was remarkable how much coal mining and its legacy was engrained in our school community. I had a part in the play *Children of the Dark* that depicted the 1838 Silkstone mining disaster. The play was performed at the Civic Theatre in Barnsley and I remember being under the spotlight and delivering my lines with members of the audience sobbing because the story I was telling of a young girl being killed in the disaster was so moving. I was part of the book in a day project and was very proud when it gained national attention. I remember singing in Westminster Abbey and really believing that perhaps it might make a difference and help our community when it was facing the closure of the pit. When the film company came to film *Brassed Off* it highlighted, once again, that our identity was knitted with the pits and the legacy of the pit closures.

Neil Kinnock once visited Willowgarth and I was allowed to shake hands with him. He made a comment about being surprised that girls were allowed to wear trousers as part of the school's uniform. I must have been quite politically aware because I remember being disappointed that the once leader of the Labour Party didn't say anything more inspiring than that. Elizabeth Peacock MEP also visited the school and held a focus group that I was part of. I remember being intrigued by her comments about 'Europe' – something I knew very little about. My sphere of experience was Barnsley. Anything else was unimaginable. We had an Entrepreneurship competition at school where we had to work in teams to design a product and market it. A rival team came up with an idea to market their product for a French market. I was gob-smacked and totally impressed by their slogan 'C'est une bonne idee!' It was so exotic!

One of the experiences that made me realize that there may be opportunities outside Barnsley was the visit my friend Julia and I made to the Houses of Parliament. We won a competition at school to write a report on the school's International Women's Day. I recall being particularly proud of my use of Lloyd Grossman's MasterChef slogan 'deliberating, cogitating and digesting' catchphrase. I guess there must have been a cooking competition as part of the day's celebrations. I remember shopping for a suitably serious outfit and being uncomfortable but excited on the train journey to London. We were given a tour of the House of Commons and House of Lords and I was in awe. Politicians that I'd watched on TV were wandering around and the historical figures I'd studied were depicted in paintings and sculptures all around. My dad had told me to shake hands with Dennis Skinner if I saw him but he was talking with Ken Livingstone and I was too shy to interrupt.

We had lunch in the Strangers' Dining Room and I remember struggling to eat it as it was smoked salmon, something I'd never really eaten before. I was completely inspired by everything I experienced that day. For the next few years I considered studying

One of Kate Dalton's father's favourites: Dennis Skinner with Rodney Bickerstaffe.
Photograph by courtesy of Rodney Bickerstaffe – with Dennis Skinner

Politics at university. In the end I opted for History but my specialist subject became Edwardian British politics. Now, I'm a History teacher. In a strange turn of events one of the students I taught when working in Northumberland recently gave me another tour of the Houses of Parliament. He works there now as a secretary to the Conservative MP for Hexham.

I currently work as Curriculum Area Leader for Social Studies at an international school in Zurich, Switzerland. It's a complete contrast to Willowgarth. The school teaches children from 55 different countries and they have all the resources and opportunities they could possibly wish for. Many of the children speak three, four and even five languages and nearly all are involved in school sports or extra-curricular clubs. In the three years that I have worked there I have been lucky enough to take advantage of many opportunities that would just not have been possible in Grimethorpe. I have taken

SOUTHBANK CENTRE

Mel Dyke
56 Limes Avenue
Staincross. Barnsley
S Yorks S75 6JT
United Kingdom

Southbank Centre · T +44 (0)20 7960 4200
Belvedere Road · F +44 (0)20 7921 0607
London · contact@southbankcentre.co.uk
SE1 8XX · www.southbankcentre.co.uk

2 October, 2012

Dear Mel,

I am writing following a letter of support I sent to you 17 years ago for the girls of Grimethorpe on the occasion of International Women's Day.

Today, women's rights and equality are as crucial a topic as they were in 1995. Issues surrounding equality in key areas such as careers, family life, law and legislation, health, sexuality, children and childcare, education and finance, among many others, are still consistent concerns for women globally.

In 2012, women are certainly more visible in positions of power, yet in the UK women only make up 15% of directors in FTSE 100 companies, there are only 144 female MPs compared to 505 male MPs, and unemployment and cuts in public spending are affecting women disproportionately.

These daily battles for equality in our society are part of what inspired me to launch the WOW – Women of the World Festival at Southbank Centre in London. The WOW Festival launched in London in 2011 as a celebration of the accomplishments of women, and as a means of exploring and challenging the obstacles preventing women from reaching their full potential.

As one of a relatively small number of women at the top of a large organisation, and as an individual, I consider it a vital part of my work to promote equality. I believe that the societies we live in will only fully flourish if women and girls are participating and engaging equally with men in all spheres.

However, what excites me is that women are responding to this challenge in greater numbers than ever before, supporting and inspiring one another to achieve their goals. There is still an enormous amount work to be done, but the enthusiasm and willingness of women and men to discuss practical ways forward has never been stronger. Feminism today still simply means a belief in equal rights and opportunities for women, and I hope the girls of Grimethorpe will continue to fight the good fight.

Warmest wishes,

Jude Kelly

Jude Kelly, OBE
Artistic Director

Still supporting local girls and women with her WOW factor, Jude Kelly revives her encouragement in 2012.

three History classes to Paris so they could spend a long weekend studying the French Revolution. I run the school's Model United Nations team and we have debated world issues with 700 other students at the UNESCO building in Paris. I have accompanied our Global Issues Network club to Luxembourg to present to 40 other international schools on the pressing environmental, societal and economic issues of today. The crown prince of Norway came to my classroom to talk to my students about dignity and being an active citizen of the world. In September 2012 I organized a day of events in Zurich for our whole upper school to celebrate International Peace Day. The founder of Peace One Day, film director Jeremy Gilley was so impressed by our efforts on the day that he flew to our school to attend our 'Uprooted and Stateless' Global Issues conference. Last year I went on a 'Classroom Without Walls' trip to Istanbul with forty students to study the history of the Ottoman Empire. This year I'll go to Beijing for a week with twenty students to study Chinese culture and history.'

Jude Kelly following up their progress in 2012 would, no doubt, be as proud of her as I am.

Yorkshire stand-up comic Billy Pearce is best known for his stage, club and TV appearances or for his extensive involvements in fundraising for

Taking time out during and after a stint in a Barnsley Night Club in the 1992, Billy Pearce was a great alternative, hard working role model for boys in Grimethorpe. By kind permission of Billy Pearce

191

local charities. His annual starring performance is a top feature of Bradford Lyceum's panto and this year again he had not only every youngster but also Calendar Girl Lynda Logan and the man who really took the photographs for that mind blowing charity fundraising calendar, husband Terry Logan in stitches. Pearce's range takes him across the comedy spectrum including adult humour which may not sound like an obvious role model for a successful career in teaching but he has far more strings to his bow than that. It was first his TV series *You gotta be joking* then his appearance on the 1991 Royal Variety Performance which caught my eye and that of young aspiring comics in Grimethorpe.

Nathan King was one whose talents offered alternatives:

'"Eh when I wor a lad" l suppose growing up and being schooled in "Grimey" the home of coal and the famous brass band I should remember the hard times, the inevitable future of working down the pit, the pit closures and the pain that surrounded this. But ever since middle school the memories I have are the complete opposite of this grim outlook, they all include sparkle and magic. Not because it wasn't happening, but because of my experiences and the people around me at that time, both at home and at school. Firstly the family values passed on to me were second to none and I couldn't get away without mentioning my long since passed gran, she was always enthusiastic and supportive of all my passions, never football, but the Arts, a dangerous thing to like if you were from Grimey. But my passion they were and who would have thought that these passions in this area could have been supported so well at that time, as they continue to be today for many others like me. I remember being sat in a cold science lab at "Big school" scared and nervous and the teacher calling to the front, me and my mate Darren, what had we done? The teacher in question was Mr Ardron as usual building the suspense, "I saw you both in plays at middle school you were great and I have written this little play about life in Barnsley in the War called *Eh when I wor a lad* and I would like you both to be in it".

Well nerves quickly turned to excitement; it wasn't going to be that bad here after all. My passion for drama started at Milefield Middle school where I can only remember rehearsing for or taking part in plays such as *Joseph and the Amazing Technicolor Dreamcoat*. The hall was the classroom, with now local hero Shaun Dooley playing Joseph he was a few years above me, I was Pharaoh, I was a tiny first year again and luckily someone dropped out and I stepped in, what a way to develop your confidence, the level of production and passion and professionalism from the teachers was amazing and something that stays with me to this day. Well that was it we had caught the bug and there was nothing we felt we couldn't do. From being asked to perform comedy sketches we "developed" from shows and TV we were always on stage and performed for parent's evenings and school events, truly supported and motivated by all staff even performing to a sell-out crowd at the Barnsley Civic. What a fantastic school it was, always recognising and motivating any ideas we had, this didn't reflect what you heard on TV about this area?

Then summoned to the deputy heads office just as ominous a prospect as it is today, we got some news! Mrs Dyke had arranged for us to go and see Billy Pearce. A "real life famous person", he'd even been on the telly. No doom and gloom but yet another door being nudged open by people who cared, people from Grimey. Well that was it, it was all we could talk about, all our hard work was paying off and people did care, even famous people cared about us and were prepared to talk to us and help. The fact that we were in a bar and we were only 14 had nothing to do with it, well maybe a little, but we were to be trusted in an environment that was usually out of bounds. I remember being really nervous but Billy was great and rather than leaving us to watch the act interacted with us and made us feel part of night. We met him back stage and had a 1000 questions to ask but were a little nervous. We met at the bar like professionals and talked for what seemed to be hours, he made us feel like the world was ours for the taking and all we had to do was grab it. That would be a far cry from the option of darn pit or darn pit.

All this was developing from the people, the teachers who cared and took notice, who fed passion; they motivated me ready for the future. Theatre was always there but in different guises and although we are not now a famous double act the performance lives on. I took part in John Kelly's Barnsley mystery plays playing Adam and designing and painting the set while studying theatre design and art at A level, then I studied Contemporary Art at Nottingham Trent before studying theatre design at Bretton Hall college once again back bouncing back to this area to study. From face painting at M&S to designing sets for a touring theatre in Sheffield and developing links with the Performing Arts Development Service in Barnsley it reignited my passion for education. I had taken part in their plays as a young lad and was asked back to support a tour of Oliver amongst other performances and to design and make the sets and costume. It was going in to schools with these shows and speaking to teachers again that made me realise I could have the same impact on the youngsters in this area the fantastic memorable inspiring impact these people had had with me.

If I could make a difference to just one person it would be worth it. If I could help inspire others in the same way I had been, then that would be the best job in the world and I would be doing what I enjoy. I have stayed in Barnsley because of these people the great people that covered the coal with magic and I hope I can follow in their footsteps. I am now teaching at Horizon CC, one of the biggest most advanced schools in the UK and this is in Barnsley. It is full of staff like the ones I remember, passionate and caring about individuals, offering fantastic opportunity to everyone. I am honoured to be a small part in what is going to be Barnsley's big future.'

Sarah Geeson was then just one more youngster involving herself in virtually every aspect of that Grimethorpe battle. She has the last word reflecting the outcome better than any of mine could:

Through my eyes.
'I had lived in the shadow of a coal mine since being born; it affected everything and also created community. The pit provided a medium for interaction between men and woman every day both socially and through work, it provided jobs, structure and stability for families despite its struggle. So when the announcement came that the pit was to close in Grimethorpe it was apparent that the effects of this decision would be far reaching and would also impact upon the schools of those communities (one of these schools I was part of), and so united in our plight we were driven (with the help of Mel) determined to have a say about the effects this would have on our community.

We spoke, wrote and displayed our feelings so we could be heard across the country. Our hearts were worn on our sleeves and we stood together united. Sadly we could not win this battle though, the decision to close the pit was final, and it was soul destroying, especially for the men who worked there and their families.

Within months of the announcement the coal industry as we knew it was gone, changing forever the future of the community and the kids in and around the surrounding areas with it. After that, it was a difficult time for the community the loss of the pit put such a huge weight on people's lives and as children, we felt it too, coal didn't just run deep underground it ran in the veins of the men that mined it.

The campaign though taught me a lot about how to stand up for what I believe and to never give up. I have had to use these skills time and time again, the letters of support the school receive made it possible to move on we were not alone and this somehow made me more resilient, more able to face a challenge despite losing the battle. For me in any case I feel as an adult that I grew as a person by experiencing it, it was a difficult time, and in a difficult time we felt proud we had tried our best we could do no more. Simply put, for me the time during and for a number of years after the pit was closed were indeed 'the best of times and the worst of times' and they shaped me. The positive events which happened in school after that, international women's day, abseiling, writing, all helped start the slow process of rebuilding.

Twenty years since then, my husband and I now run a renewable energy business, installing greener more energy efficient technologies from Solar PV, to LED lighting and much more, and even though we have moved from one energy source to another we are still faced with some of the same struggles. No matter how we look at it our industry too is influenced by government policy. It is apparent Obstacles, U-turns and decisions made by central government will always have a direct impact on people's lives and communities, and more often than not it's the speed at which these changes are brought in that cause the most impact, people just have no time to prepare, or adapt, or to retrain, its then that people and communities suffer.

As we try to grow our business we live with the knowledge that it can take a government only a day to change an industry. It happened to us at the end of 2011 when the government made a decision to drastically cut the feed in tariff for solar pv before the end of a consultation period, this decision caused people to lose confidence, the industry was damaged and it was inevitable then that people would lose jobs.

It was a difficult time and it's been a hard road to recovery but we pressed and at least for now the industry is on a much more positive footing and is growing steadily again, but it brought it all back to me and it encompassed all that the past has taught me, to be resilient, to fight for what you believe, to survive and have hope.

I believe in this industry and can see all the positives that green energy can bring to Yorkshire and the UK like long-term jobs, job security, lower priced energy, energy stability and all the environmental benefits and I'll do my best to make it work so that my children can benefit from a more stable energy future. But like all things though, it's only as secure as the government wants it to be and so I'm ready, if the time comes again, to battle on. Coal will always be an important part of our heritage and because of it; I now believe I have enough strength to help to ensure that greener energy will play a part in its future.'

The message of the NUM's national banner.

Final Acknowledgements

The following people have in different ways been generous contributors to this book for which I am most grateful. Without their memories, creative ideas, professional advice, technological and administrative assistance, written or other inputs in support of the work, and their friendship, the events in some cases could not have taken place; and the stories would still be filed away, or lost:

The Bishop of Manchester, Nigel McCulloch
The Bishop of Wakefield, Stephen Platten
The Bishop of Sheffield, David Lunn
The Bishop of Doncaster, Peter Burrows
Catherine Bailey
Nick Balac
Susanne Bell
Lynda Bellingham
Rodney Bickerstaffe
Rev Derek Birch
Peter Birkby
Ron Blackburn
John Bostwick
Nick Bowen
Max Bristowe
Rita Britton
Rita Brown
Stephen Buckley
Keith Bunker
Dr Michael Clark
Gary Clarke
John Clegg

Peter Clegg
Glen Cook
Phil Coppard OBE
Oliver Coppard
Kate Dalton
Janet Dalton
Chris Davison
Debbie Dolan
Ann Dooley
Shaun Dooley
Michael Dugher MP
Barbara Edwards
Jeff Ennis
Wieke Eringa
Ron Fisher
Dr Joann Fletcher
John Foster MBE
Claire Garrity
Sarah Geeson
John Godber
Jane Godber
Peter Goodman
Sarah Harris
Andrew Harrod
Simon Hirst
Wes Hobson

Vera Holling
Cllr Stephen Houghton
Eric Illsley
Dan Jarvis MP
Mel Jenkinson
Don Jones
Jude Kelly
Nathan King
Lynne Kirkwood
Chris Lawton
Lynda Logan
Terry Logan
Pauline Lyon
Jayne Manley
David Markwell
Lord Mason of Barnsley
Linda McAvan MEP
Jenny Miccoli
Liz McPolin
David Moody
Philip Mosley
Terry Mullen
Jane Mullen
Gillian Nixon
Elizabeth Peacock
Billy Pearce

Rita Poole
Janet Richardson
Stan Robinson
Sharon Rossides
Joanne Tasker
Robert Teal
Phil Thompson
Marlene Sidaway
Chris Skidmore
Angela Smith MP
Tom Smith
Alison Steadman
Mike Swallow
David Thacker
Stephen Tompkinson
Mick Wadsworth
Dick Walker
Graham Walker
Chrissie Yates

Barnsley Chronicle
Yorkshire Post Newspapers
Star Newspapers
BBC Radio Sheffield
BBC Radio Leeds
Dearne FM

Additional acknowledgements of past individual involvements:

The Archbishop of
   York, David Hope
Kate Adie
Debbie Allen
Tracy Allott
Dave Ardron
Ray Ashton
Sandra Barnes
Val Barry
Marie Bedford
Jill Best

Roger Beswick
Flt Lt Nikola Bill
Brian Blessed
Bob Bone
Jackie Bone
Mo Bone
Tony Bould
Victoria Boyden
Graham Bradbury
Jane Bradshaw
Mark Britton

Sister Broadhead
Oliver Brooke
Karen Brunton
Ken Capstick
Michael Clapham MP
Barbara Clayton
Barry Cook
Betty Cook
Glen Cook
Kathleen Craggs
Andy Crothers

Final Acknowledgements

Sharon Curran
Dr Davis Reynolds
Kate Dodd
Berlie Doherty
Debbie Dolan
Dr Tony Dorney
Kenny Doughty
Betty Driver
David Duke
Derek Emms
Keith Ellis MBE
Jenny Evans
Mark Fairweather
Margaret Ferry
Les Foweather
Lesley Frances
Ed Gabbani
Brian Glover
John Godber
Jane Godber
George Gregg
Scott Haigh
Mike Hale
Dawn Hancock
Gail Hancock
Ken Hancock
Matthew Hancock
Nicholas Handley
Rebecca Hanson
Joan Hardy
Anne Harnett
Mike Hill
Janet Holland
Martin Homer
Pat Howarth
Eric Jackson
Linda Jackson
Dr Mary Jefferson
Colin Jones
Les Jones
Brigit Kane
John Kelly
Steve Kemp
Claire King
Glenys Kinnock

Ian Lavery
Gaele Levy
Andrew Livingston
Caroline Lister
Stacey Lodge
John Lomas
Maggie Loy
Sue MacGregor
Sara Maitland
Vicky Mallinson
Heather Marsh
Betty Martin
Katrina Marriott
Joanne Mason
Martin Matthews
Cheryl McCanaan
Lady McGeogh
Alan McKay
Tony McNally
Iris McNair
Rev Tony McPherson
David Meggitt
Mike Miller
Dayle Moore
Estelle Morris
Jenni Murray
Joy Nicholas
Sue Nicholls
Elizabeth North
Mary Parkinson
Michael Parkinson
Chris Parr
Terry Patchett MP
Tony Parkinson
Fiona Patterson
Christopher Peach
Jack Peach
Joan Peach
Janet Pearson
Melanie Perkins
Anne Phipps
Su Pollard
Eric Pressley
Yvonne Preston
Sue Pritchard

Barbara Rennie
Carolyn Reynolds
Hedley Salt
Sheila Salt
Anne Sanderson
Jane Sanderson
Ben Saxton
Prunella Scales
Ann Scargill
Arthur Scargill
Valerie Singleton
Darren Smith
Linda Smith
Kathy Staffe
Janet Suzman
Debra Tate
Ann Taylor
Robert Teal
Margaret Thacker
Jenny Tickle
Joan Thirkettle
Avril Todd
Claire Upton
Julia Utley
Bev Vosper
Tommy Wadsworth
Donna Ward
Sarah Walmsley
Donna White
Vicky Whitely
Colin Watson
Malcolm Warrington
Norman West MEP
John Whittington
Ron Wilby
Dave Wiles
Jo Wiles
Norman Willis
Jack Wood
Janet Wood
Annette Woodward
Sandra Woolridge
Bruna Zamelli